PRINTING IN DELAWARE

1761–1800

THE

ADVICE

Of EVAN ELLIS, late of Chester County, deceased, to
his DAUGHTER, when at Sea.

My dear and only Child,

MY Heart longs after thee, and
I am very much humbled for
fear of thy Faultering now in
thy youthful and precious Days.

Take this for my last Legacy, and
remember that it is my hearty Desire
that thou mayest redeem thy precious
Time: There is no recalling of it when
past; and it passes with a Thought.

Use thyself to Solitude, and keep thy
Mind humble before the ALMIGHTY,
with Prayers constantly Imploring him
for Grace, to preserve thee in his Fear,
to conduct, defend and protect thee a-
gainst all outward and potent Enemies,
the *World*, the *Flesh*, and the *Devil*.

Keep always a sober and settled Coun-
tenance, which will very much adorn
thee before GOD and Man.

Keep the best Company, as well as
read the best Books, and that will con-
duce much towards thy eternal Happiness.

What seemeth odious to thee in others,
be sure to avoid and refrain from thyself.

When thou goest to lie down at
Night, having strip'd thyself of thy outward Cloathing, remember that that
may be the last, and that so thou must
be also strip'd of all Things in the World,
and return naked as thou camest. Run
over the Lines of the Day past, and ob-
serve well how thou hast spent them, and
if *Well*, then return humble Thanks to
the Lord for his tender Protection; but
if there be a Remorse and Trouble in thy
Conscience, then give no Rest to thyself
'till thou hast Peace with GOD in thyself.

In the Morning when thou arisest,
pray to the Lord for his Assistance and
Protection every Hour of the Day 'till
thou layest down thyself again; and so
continue all the Days of thy Life, that
thou mayest *be happy in thy End, to rest
from thy Labour, and thy good Works will
follow thee.*

Keep thyself Chaste, as well thy Mind
as thy Body.

Be curious and desirous, in time, to
know for what End GOD created thee;
and if it please him to call thee to his
Service, see that thou be ready to answer his *Call*, as *Samuel* did in Time of
old; so shall the LORD delight in thee,
and the Angel of his Presence will go
along with thee, and neither *Death* nor
Hell shall have Power against thee, nor
terrify thee.

Let thy Words be few, solid and con-
siderate; the LORD hath given thee Wit
and Sense enough, *my dear Child*, do not
make bad Use of it to thy Condemna-
tion, the Consequence of which is Hor-
ror and Amazement, that will suddenly
overtake them that neglect their Duty
towards so Merciful a GOD.

Be careful to attend thy Meetings,
and when thou sits, remember before
whose tremendous Presence thou dost
appear, and for what End thou camest,
even to worship the Great JEHOVAH,
that made thee and all the World, won-
derful in Being.

Put off childish Things, and appear
meek, modest, and gentle to thy Equals
and Superiors.

Envy no Body, nor disturb thy Mind
about little Trifles and Humours, whose
Products are Vexations.

Thee must know, *my Darling*, that
with many Tears I wrote these few Precepts to thee, amongst a Tumult, and
upon the ingurgitating Waves tossing to
and fro, so that I can neither write nor
indite to my Mind. I desire thee not
to neglect them, but read them often,
and write them over plainer than I can
at present.

Go and see thy Grand-Mother often,
and comfort her in her old Age, that
thou mayest expect the same if Age
should overtake thee: For the Merciful shall obtain Mercy.---Give my kind
Love to her.

Be obedient to thy dear Mother, and
take her Advice, for she hath known
much of the Disappointments of this
World.

Time hastens me to draw to a Conclu-
sion: The LORD GOD Almighty, under whose Government all Things are
disposed, bless thee with Faith unspot-
ted, and Patience to run through this
dangerous World, and give thee at
last Admittance into the Mansion of
Glory.

Farewel, my dear Child, farewel.

From thy tender Father,

EVAN ELLIS.

2d Mo. 14th Day, 1740.

To LYDIA ELLIS, *jun.*
These present.

WILMINGTON, Printed by JAMES ADAMS, at his PRINTING-OFFICE,
in *Market-street.*

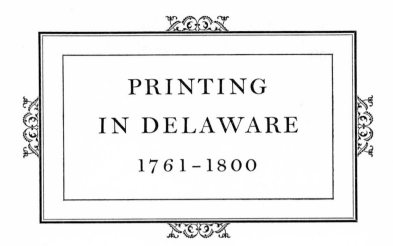

PRINTING
IN DELAWARE
1761–1800

A Checklist by EVALD RINK

1969

Eleutherian Mills Historical Library

Wilmington, Delaware

FIRST PUBLISHED 1969
COPYRIGHT © 1969 BY THE ELEUTHERIAN MILLS-HAGLEY FOUNDATION
LIBRARY OF CONGRESS CATALOG CARD NUMBER: 76-96058
PRINTED IN THE UNITED STATES OF AMERICA
AT THE STINEHOUR PRESS

CONTENTS

ILLUSTRATIONS

FOREWORD

THE NEED for a checklist of eighteenth century Delaware imprints has been felt for some time. The impetus to compile such a list came a few years ago from the Council of Historical Libraries of Delaware, which engaged Mr. Richard C. Quick, then at the Library of the University of Delaware, to undertake this task. Before he could make much progress, Mr. Quick left Delaware and the present compiler was charged with the completion of the checklist.

It was then decided to make this list as comprehensive as possible and to supplement it with an introductory essay on the printers of Delaware. Guidelines for the bibliographical description of the imprints were agreed upon. According to these, the titles are given with sufficient completeness for their identification. Lengthy titles are frequently abbreviated, but the omissions are indicated. Capitalization and punctuation, the latter particularly in imprint information, follow modern library practice. Spelling, however, conforms to the text of the title page or that of the bibliographical source. Imprint year is always given in Arabic numerals. The format of the publications is indicated rather than the size in centimeters.

Whenever possible the entries have references to bibliographical sources where they have been previously recorded. Through the cooperation of the American Antiquarian Society, numbers (above Evans 39162) have been supplied for those items which are listed in Roger P. Bristol's forthcoming supplement to Evans' *American Bibliography*.

7

Not all items in this checklist could be located. Doubtful publications have been included and annotated if clarifying information was available. All known Delaware locations have been given, and the holdings of some major depositories such as the American Antiquarian Society, the Library of Congress and the Library Company of Philadelphia are completely covered. No attempt was made to give all locations, except in cases when no more than three are known. The newspaper holdings of individual libraries have not been recorded in detail; the location symbol indicates only that the respective library has at least one issue of that particular year.

The help and cooperation received from many individuals and institutions, too numerous to list, have been most generous and are here thankfully acknowledged. This assistance has greatly increased the completeness and usefulness of the checklist; any omissions and inaccuracies that still remain are solely the responsibility of the compiler. And, finally, without the support and encouragement of Dr. Richmond D. Williams, Director of the Eleutherian Mills Historical Library, this checklist would not have been completed.

E.R.

INTRODUCTION

ORIGINALLY settled by the Dutch, the Swedes and the Finns, the territory of the present state of Delaware became a part of the British holdings in the New World during the last half of the seventeenth century. The William Penn Charter of 1681 made no reference to Delaware because it was then held by the Duke of York. Upon Penn's petition, the Duke ceded this area to Penn in 1682. It was known during colonial times as the Three Lower Counties, or the Counties on the Delaware.

A separate legislature for the government of this area was obtained in 1704, but strong political and economic ties with Pennsylvania continued. Even after the present state of Delaware was created in 1776, this area retained, as a legacy from the days of Penn, close social and economic relations with Pennsylvania, particularly with the city of Philadelphia.

Delaware offered little to attract printers. Its population was small, estimated to be only a little over 35,000 in 1774.[1] It was predominantly rural with few urban settlements. The town of New Castle grew out of an early Dutch settlement on the Delaware River and served as the seat of the colonial government for the Three Lower Counties. During the Revolution, the government of the state of Delaware was moved to Dover in 1777. New Castle continued as the administrative center of New Castle County until 1881, when Wilmington took its

---

1. Stella H. Sutherland, *Population Distribution in Colonial America* (New York, AMS Press, 1966), p. 135.

place. It remained a small town and had probably not more than five hundred inhabitants in the middle of the eighteenth century. Wilmington, the largest Delaware town, was founded in 1731 near the first Swedish settlement on the Christina River. Its growth during the eighteenth century was slow. In 1735 it consisted of some fifteen or twenty houses. In 1739 it had 610 inhabitants, and by 1800 the population of Wilmington had increased to only 3,241. There were no notable educational institutions in Delaware, and the number of professional residents was rather small. The market for the printed word was, therefore, very limited and could hardly support local printers.

Philadelphia, the largest city in colonial America, was about thirty miles away and was easily accessible by coach or boat. It early became the most significant center of printing in America. William Bradford established a press there in 1685;[2] he was followed by several others, including Benjamin Franklin. For many years the needs of Delaware were satisfied by the Philadelphia printers. Philadelphia newspapers and magazines were circulated in Delaware; almanacs, books, pamphlets and any kind of job-printing also came from there. Even the printing of Delaware laws and other official publications was done in Philadelphia. It is, therefore, not surprising that printing started later in Delaware than in any of the other thirteen original states, except Georgia. Printing presses and type were expensive and had to be imported from Europe. Until the substantial investment in equipment could be justified, there had to be some assurance that the public would

2. Douglas C. McMurtrie, *A History of Printing in the United States* (New York, Bowker, 1936), II, [1].

10

support such enterprises. Not before 1761 was a printer prepared to take the gamble in Delaware.

The record of printing and publishing reflects in many ways the cultural, political and business life of a community. Delaware's case during the eighteenth century emerges as a relatively unexciting one. What happened there had mainly local significance. The whole area was overshadowed by more populous and energetic neighbors. The number of printers who established themselves in Delaware during this period was small. Few of them have gained prominence, and information about most of them is quite fragmentary and frequently unreliable. Their careers are discussed below in the order of their appearance in the state.

* * *

Sometime before 1753 a young Irishman, James Adams,[3] arrived in Philadelphia. He was born about 1725 in Londonderry where he probably learned the trade of the printer. He was connected with the Philadelphia printing firm of Franklin and Hall for seven years. Adams claimed to have worked at the printing press with Benjamin Franklin. This seems unlikely since Franklin took no part in actual printing after the formation of his partnership with David Hall in 1748.

Adams was married to Martha Keith Henry in Christ Church in Philadelphia, probably in 1753. About the year 1760 he set up his own business, possibly with money received from his wife. He soon realized that competition with

3. The account of his life and career is largely based on Dorothy L. Hawkins' "James Adams, the First Printer of Delaware," *Papers of the Bibliographical Society of America*, XXVIII (1934), p. 28–63.

a dozen or more established printers and booksellers in Philadelphia was too keen. In his search for a more promising location he disregarded Franklin's advice that he settle in the British West Indies. Instead, Adams chose Delaware, a virgin field not far away. It was a wise choice. He prospered and remained in business in Wilmington as an esteemed citizen for thirty-one years.

He advertised his move to Delaware in the *Pennsylvania Gazette* of September 24, 1761, and opened a printing office and bookshop in Wilmington on lower Market Street. Sometime in 1774 he moved his business to High (now Fourth) Street. Relatively little is known about James Adams' private life in Wilmington. William McCulloch, who supplied Isaiah Thomas with additional information on early printing, reported that Adams was the father of ten children,[4] but only four sons and three daughters are known.[5] At least three of his sons, James, Samuel and John, later became printers and will be mentioned below.

James Adams carried on his trade in Wilmington undisturbed until the American Revolution. As a supporter of the patriot cause, he felt compelled to leave the town as the British approached on their way to Philadelphia, probably in Sep-

4. William McCulloch, "William McCulloch's Additions to Thomas's History of Printing," *American Antiquarian Society Bulletin*, n.s., xxxi (1921), p. 132.

5. The eldest son of James Adams, Hans, had been in the Revolutionary War and died in Wilmington of "camp fever." He also may have been active as a printer, but no samples of his work are known. James Adams' other sons, James, John and Samuel, became printers. One daughter, Sarah, died February 7, 1766, when she was seven years old. Martha, born four or five years before her, later married the respected Wilmington innkeeper, Captain Patrick O'Flinn, and died in 1779 when she was only twenty-five years old. Adams' youngest daughter, Mary, married Rev. Robert Keith, a graduate of Princeton, who served as a chaplain during the Revolutionary War and died in 1784. Mary Keith was still living when her father died in 1792.

tember of 1777. His activities as the official printer of Delaware, particularly the printing of paper currency, may have been the main factor in his decision to remove beyond the reach of the British.

Together with his family, press and stock, he moved north to the vicinity of Doylestown in Pennsylvania. He is supposed to have printed an almanac there, the *Pennsylvania and Country-Man's Almanack* for 1778, compiled by John Tobler, but no copy of it has been found. Adams returned to Wilmington after the British had left Philadelphia in June of 1778. During the war years he issued a few political pamphlets and broadsides; but he used his press less than most other patriotic printers of the period to express his own sympathies and to promote the idea of American independence, nor did he become involved in local political affairs.

With no competition in business until 1785, James Adams prospered. He was well liked in the community and was considered a good workman and an honest citizen. He died in Wilmington on December 11, 1792. The *Pennsylvania Gazette* for December 29 published the following obituary:

Wilmington, December 15.—Died last Tuesday morning, in the 68th year of his age, Mr. James Adams, printer, and on Thursday afternoon his remains were interred in the Presbyterian Grave yard; as he was a useful member of the Society. His funeral was attended by a great concourse of the inhabitants of this place, and of the neighbourhood around; as he was highly esteemed, by all who knew him, for the benevolence of his disposition, the inoffensiveness of his behaviour, and the purity of his manners.

He has lived for many years in this borough, and was always diligent in business and remarkable for the regularity, neatness, and correctness of his printing. It may be truly said, that he discharged the several duties of his station, with attention, punctuality and fidelity; and that he was, in reality, a good citizen—an honest man—and a pious Christian.

His will, probated in New Castle County, Delaware, on January 7, 1793, indicates that he left considerable property, including two houses and several building lots in Wilmington. He also owned the presses and stock of two printing shops, one of which was at that time operated in Baltimore by his sons John and Samuel. He was buried in the Presbyterian Cemetery. His grave was later moved to the Wilmington and Brandywine Cemetery where the marker can be seen today.

After coming to Delaware in 1761, James Adams printed four items in the fall of that year. According to an advertisement in the *Pennsylvania Gazette*, November 5, 1761, these were: 1. *The Wilmington Almanack* for the year 1762, by Thomas Fox; 2. *The Child's New Spelling-Book*; 3. *The Merchant and Trader's Security*; and 4. *The Advice of Evan Ellis*. Of these, the almanac and the spelling book were small pamphlets, *The Merchant and Trader's Security* was probably a book of some size and the last was a broadside. Only the almanac and the broadside are known to have survived, the last in one copy only.

Because no copy of *The Child's New Spelling-Book* is known to exist, there is disagreement about its exact title. Charles Evans has listed it in his *American Bibliography* as *The Child's New Play-Thing, or Best Amusement, Being a Spelling-Book*.[6] An advertisement in Fox's *Wilmington Almanack* for 1762 confirms the form the title had in the advertisement in the *Pennsylvania Gazette*, and Hildeburn lists it in the same way

6. Charles Evans, *The American Bibliography* (New York, P. Smith, 1941–1959), no. 8813.

in *A Century of Printing. The Issues of the Press in Pennsylvania, 1685–1784.*[7] Dorothy Hawkins in "James Adams, the First Printer of Delaware" was inclined to accept this, rather than the Evans' version, as the correct title.[8] The completeness of the title given by Evans differed substantially from the text in advertisements which probably were known to Evans. This suggests that he had seen a copy or had received a description of this publication. A few years earlier, a publication with an identical title had been issued by James Chattin, a Philadelphia printer.[9]

The Child's New Play-Thing has attracted considerable attention because it was once considered to be the first book printed in Delaware. There seems to be no reason for assigning priority to this title over the other three; it is only the first imprint mentioned by Hildeburn and by Evans, since the arrangement of their lists, under each year, is alphabetical. Comparison of the advertisements in the *Pennsylvania Gazette* and Fox's *Wilmington Almanack* indicates that the almanac was issued after *The Child's New Play-Thing*. Not until copies of all four 1761 imprints have been located can a plausible sequence of publication be established. It seems reasonable to assume that a printer, having set up a new press, would first try out his equipment by issuing some simple publication such as a broadside. If this is true, *The Advice of Evan Ellis* may be the earliest sample of printing in Delaware.

During the next year, James Adams printed another issue of Fox's *Almanack*, a religious pamphlet, *Daily Conversations*

7. Charles R. Hildeburn, *A Century of Printing. The Issues of the Press in Pennsylvania, 1685–1784* (Philadelphia, 1886), no. 1718.

8. Hawkins, p. 34.

9. Evans, no. 7871.

with God and *Votes and Proceedings of the House of Representatives* for 1762. He established himself with the latter work as the public printer of Delaware. In 1762 he also issued a more ambitious work, Thomas Dilworth's *A New Guide to the English Tongue*, the first book printed in Delaware of which copies are still in existence. James Adams would have been a rare exception among colonial printers if he had not attempted to issue a newspaper. The assumption that he did so in 1762 rests on the statement of Isaiah Thomas in his *History of Printing in America*:

> The first and only newspaper published before 1775, in what is now the state of Delaware, made its appearance in Wilmington about the year 1761, entitled, if my information is correct, *The Wilmington Courant*. Printed and published by James Adams, for the short period of six months; when, for want of encouragement, it was discontinued.[10]

Thomas was not sure about his information because in his general account of printing in Delaware he claimed that "in 1762, he [Adams] published 'Proposals for printing a news paper'; but not meeting with encouragement, it was discontinued after being published six months."[11] In the second edition of Thomas' *History of Printing*, published after his death, which includes the manuscript corrections made by him for a projected revised edition, this statement was changed to state that the *Wilmington Courant* was printed and published by James Adams in 1762 for a period of six months. No copy of this newspaper or of the proposal to print it has been discovered; and, consequently, the beginnings of newspaper pub-

10. Isaiah Thomas, *The History of Printing in America* (Worcester, I. Thomas, 1810), II, 349.
11. *Ibid.*, II, 125–6.

lishing in Delaware are still shrouded in doubt. Thomas added that about the year 1787 Adams began the publication of another paper, also entitled the *Wilmington Courant*, which he issued for two or three years.[12]

During Adams' third year in business, he printed a two volume set of Delaware laws. It has been generally believed that in 1763 Adams brought out only the second volume of the *Laws of the Government of New Castle, Kent and Sussex, upon Delaware* as a continuation of an earlier compilation of Delaware laws passed prior to 1752 and printed in Philadelphia by Franklin and Hall.[13] Recently a copy of the first volume was located at the Peabody Institute in Baltimore. This proves that the Wilmington, 1763, edition was a new, complete work and covered all Delaware laws passed up to that year.

The works printed by James Adams during the years that followed were fairly similar to the output of other good colonial printers. He published two almanacs for many years, one compiled by Thomas Fox, the other by John Tobler, religious tracts and some useful handbooks and educational works. Official printing, such as the laws and the proceedings of the legislative bodies, was a particularly important part of his work. Occasional proclamations, advertisements, many kinds of legal forms and bills of sale were also printed and sold in the owner's shop. James Adams was known to his contemporaries as a pious man. This may partially explain

---

12. Isaiah Thomas, *The History of Printing in America*, 2d ed. (Albany, J. Munsell, 1874), II, 154. Thomas made a mistake in the title of the last paper which should read the *Delaware Courant*. It was not printed and published by James Adams, but by his sons Samuel and John.

13. Hawkins, p. 37.

the large number of moral and religious publications which he issued. Among these were the *New Testament* in 1781 and a reprint of three fundamental Quaker tracts in 1783 issued under the title, *Three Treatises . . . the First by William Penn, in England; the Second by Robert Barclay, in Scotland; and the Third by Joseph Pike, in Ireland.* The parts of the latter work have separate title pages, but the whole appears to have been printed as one work because the signature numbering is continuous. Religious works were the best sellers of the period; that Adams printed so many of them indicates a good judgment of popular demand.

Only a few secular works issued by Adams were important publications. A rather popular book was *The Citizen and Countryman's Experienced Farrier* which he issued in 1764. John Millis, a farrier living in Chester County, Pennsylvania, extracted the text of this publication from an old work written by Gervase Markham in England more than a hundred years before. In 1784 James Adams published probably the most notable of his imprints, *The Discovery, Settlement and Present State of Kentucke* by John Filson, a former Delawarean. This is the first geographical account of Kentucky, including notes on the Indians and an account of the adventures of Colonel Daniel Boone. It was accompanied by a map of Kentucky made by Filson in consultation with the early pioneers of the region. It is not known whether Filson selected Adams as the printer because of a former aquaintanceship or merely because Adams offered more favorable terms than printers in other towns. The map was engraved in Philadelphia by Henry D. Purcell and printed there by Ternor Rook because Adams had no facilities for such a work. It seems that the book and the map were sold either together or separately. This work is regarded as one of the most important documents on the western expansion of the United States; for this reason Filson's life and explorations, as well as his book and map, have been described in several studies.[14]

Official printing was an important part of James Adams' business. He had no competition until 1785; most of the state publications of this, and all of the succeeding year, carry the imprint of Jacob A. Killen & Co. of Wilmington. From 1788 until the end of his printing career in 1792, James Adams again had a fair share in the official Delaware printing; and after his death, his sons, John and Samuel, controlled about the same proportion of it.

During his many years as a Wilmington printer, Adams was assisted by many apprentices and workmen to whom he taught his trade. These included first of all his sons, James, John and Samuel, and possibly also his eldest son, Hans. Some of those whom he had taught to print were later independent printers. Jacob A. Killen, the second printer in Delaware and Adams' first competitor, probably learned his trade from him. Isaac Collins, a native of Delaware who later became an important printer in New Jersey, served his apprenticeship with Adams,[15] as did another New Jersey printer, Shepard Kollock.[16] There were certainly many others because

14. Filson was born in Chester County, Pennsylvania, and served in Wilmington as a schoolteacher before going West. For his life see Reuben T. Durrett, *John Filson, the First Historian of Kentucky* (Louisville, The Filson Club, 1884), and the introduction by Willard R. Jillson in the facsimile edition of John Filson's *Kentucke* (Louisville, J. P. Morton, 1929).

15. Richard F. Hixon, *Isaac Collins; a Quaker Printer in 18th Century America* (New Brunswick, Rutgers Univ. Press, 1968), p. 6–11.

16. McMurtrie, II, 236.

his advertisements for apprentices are found at intervals in the newspapers. One of them was still running in the *Delaware Gazette* when he died late in 1792. There is evidence that during periods of slack business he loaned his assistants to Philadelphia printers, particularly to Mathew Carey.[17] He also used Philadelphia booksellers as an outlet for his products especially during the early years of his career. At the same time, in his shop he sold books from other American printers, particularly those of Philadelphia, as well as publications imported from England.

As the first printer in Delaware, James Adams holds an important position in the history of printing in the United States. He was active in Wilmington for almost a third of a century. Although there are only a few notable publications among his imprints, the general quality of his printing is comparable with the production of his best contemporaries. He was no innovator, but was a skilled craftsman with good taste. Adams' competitors and successors in Delaware during the eighteenth century were not able to improve upon the quality of his printing. Of the 566 known publications issued by the Delaware printers before 1801, 235 carry the imprint of James Adams. Together with the output from the presses of the sons, the Adams family was responsible for more than half of the printing done in Delaware during the eighteenth century.

* * *

Three sons, James, Samuel and John Adams, decided early to follow their father's footsteps. They were all engaged in

17. Hawkins, p. 55.

printing several years before his death. Six items issued during 1788 and 1789 carry the imprint of James Adams and Sons. In 1793, after the death of their father, the sons apparently kept his shop operating, using the imprint "Adams's Press" on at least three publications.

Samuel may have ventured first into the printing field. A broadside entitled *A Mournful Lamentation on the Untimely Death of Paper Money*, known only through a photocopy in the New York Public Library,[18] carries the following imprint: "Printed by Sam. Adams, in the 10th year of his age, and 1st month of his apprenticeship, 1781." It has been considered a Boston imprint, but no Samuel Adams is known to have been a printer in Boston before 1800. This sheet could be considered tentatively as an early example of the work of Samuel Adams of Wilmington. The question may be solved when the date of his birth is discovered.

Not until 1786 did the Adams brothers seriously start their independent careers. On May 17, James and Samuel issued a notice of their proposal to establish a newspaper in Wilmington called the *Delaware Courant*. For some reason this newspaper, when it started later that year, was published jointly, not by James and Samuel, but by Samuel and John Adams. Throughout the later printing career of the brothers, James was never associated with the other two, but worked either by himself or in partnership with Hezekiah Niles. He had his printing shop on the "north side of the Upper Market," or "opposite the Upper Market," on what is now Fourth Street in Wilmington. Only a few samples of his work are known.

18. The original was sold at the American Art Association sale in New York, January 31, 1921, to an unidentified buyer.

These include *The Millenium; or The Thousand Years of Prosperity, Promised by the Church of God* by David Austin, printed in 1795 according to an advertisement in the *Delaware and Eastern-Shore Advertiser; The History of Thomas Thumb,* printed in 1797; and *The United States Almanac* for the years 1796 to 1799 and for 1801. The almanacs for 1796 and 1797 were published in partnership with Hezekiah Niles. No publications with the imprint of James Adams are known after 1800. He moved to Philadelphia about 1802 and was still living there in 1814 when William McCulloch wrote his notes to Isaiah Thomas.[19]

Samuel and John Adams began their partnership by issuing a weekly newspaper in Wilmington entitled the *Delaware Courant, and Wilmington Advertiser.* Their printing shop was located at the corner of King and High Streets. Judging from the date of the earliest known issue (vol. 1, no. 35, May 5, 1787), this newspaper was established in September of 1786. Only a few issues of it have survived. The *Delaware Courant* was published concurrently with Jacob Killen's *Delaware Gazette.* It was not successful in competition and was probably discontinued soon after September 8, 1787, the date of the last known issue.

The two brothers continued their business in Wilmington at least until 1799. During this time they had secured for themselves a share of the state printing, issuing the journals of the Delaware House of Representatives and of the Senate for the years 1793 to 1796. They also printed instructions in French for the pronunciation of the English language, apparently for the use of refugees from the French colony of Saint

19. Hawkins, p. 31.

Domingue. Several almanacs, compiled by Thomas Fox and Benjamin Banneker, were an important part of their business. They also printed a number of religious works; some of them, like William Duke's *A Clew to Religious Truth*, were works of considerable size. A new type of reading material, light fiction and adventure stories, was now printed on a Delaware press by John and Samuel Adams for the first time. These included *The History of Louisa, the Lovely Orphan* by Elizabeth Helme and *An Account of the Pelew Islands* by George Keate.

Samuel and John Adams, looking for ways to develop a profitable business, realized in the late 1780's that Delaware did not offer a large enough market. They had several active competitors by that time which considerably reduced their opportunities. While continuing to operate in Wilmington, they opened another printing shop and bookstore in Baltimore in 1789, probably with financial support from their father. Their shop in Baltimore was located on Market Street between South and Gay Streets and later at the corner of Gay and Second Streets. About twenty publications with their Baltimore imprint are known to have been issued from 1789 to 1795. The general character of these is similar to their Wilmington work. Several of the religious tracts they printed in Baltimore concern the Swedenborgian Church; others discuss the religious problems in Maryland, particularly of the Roman Catholic Church. Certain almanacs for this period were issued at both Wilmington and Baltimore with only the imprint differing.

The Baltimore venture did not, however, prove to be successful. The brothers abandoned it in 1795 or 1796. Using the equipment brought back from Baltimore, they established another printing shop, this time at New Castle, Delaware, then the seat of the government of New Castle County. This was the first printing press operated outside of Wilmington in Delaware. The new shop was located in the center of town, "nearly opposite the Court-House." At this new location, the Adams brothers again managed to secure for themselves most of the Delaware official printing. The journals of the House and the Senate and the session laws for 1796 to 1800 were printed on their New Castle press. The most notable example of their work at New Castle is a two volume collection of Delaware laws issued in 1797. Altogether more than twenty publications with the Adams' New Castle imprint are known today.

During the years John and Samuel Adams were printing at New Castle they also maintained their Wilmington business, but few publications were printed there. Their Wilmington press was used chiefly to print a second newspaper, the *Delaware and Eastern-Shore Advertiser*. The brothers had established this paper on May 14, 1794, in partnership with William Catherwood Smyth. In 1795 Smyth left the partnership and the two Adams brothers continued the paper until the end of 1799.

Despite the running of two presses and having practically a monopoly of official printing, John and Samuel Adams were unable to make printing a profitable business in Delaware. Again they had to look elsewhere for better opportunities. In March of 1800 they prepared to leave and advertised for sale in the Wilmington *Mirror of the Times* "a three story brick house, and large kitchen, with two or three building lots, adjoining the same, situate on the corner of King and High

Streets, Wilmington, also a two story brick house, &c., situate on the north side of the Upper Market House, Wilmington." There has been uncertainty about the next location of their business. Some have expressed the opinion that they returned to Baltimore.[20]

There is no basis for this assumption; rather it is known that soon after 1800 the brothers moved their business to Philadelphia. Earlier connections, especially with Mathew Carey, may have influenced their decision. It seems likely that the partnership of John and Samuel Adams was dissolved about the same time because no Philadelphia publications with their joint imprint are known. Samuel Adams died in the spring of 1803. The disappointments in business and financial difficulties may have contributed to the deterioration of his health.[21] The Wilmington *Mirror of the Times & General Advertiser* carried two advertisements on April 6 of the same year, one calling for the settlement of debts against the estate of Samuel Adams and the other announcing the sale of his real estate, household goods and printing equipment in Wilmington.

The Philadelphia directories for the years 1803 through 1812 list John Adams as a printer, first at Twelfth Street near Locust, and then at the corner of Walnut and Eleventh Streets. It is not known whether he did any printing in Philadelphia before 1802, but during this year he issued at least four publications, three of them almanacs. In Philadelphia,

20. Henry C. Conrad, *History of the State of Delaware* (Wilmington, 1908), p. 1086.
21. It is known that Samuel Adams had become a drinker during the last years of his life. Mason Locke Weems wrote to Mathew Carey on March 27, 1802: "Poor Samuel Adams, who is at my elbow and most troublesomely drunk . . ." Cf. Mason L. Weems, *Mason Locke Weems, his Works and Ways* (New York, 1929), I, 269.

John Adams seemed to prefer the printing of works with a potential mass market, such as almanacs, schoolbooks and religious tracts. He remained in constant financial difficulties. Mason Locke Weems—for whom Adams had formerly printed a few books and for which Weems still owed him money—repeatedly urged Mathew Carey to have some of his printing done by John Adams.[22]

John Adams conducted his printing business in Philadelphia at least until 1812. No publications with his name are known after that year. When William McCulloch visited him in 1814 to discuss the printing career of his father, James Adams, John was held in the debtors' prison in Philadelphia and was, together with his brother James, "in the worst position of worldly goods."[23] John died in Philadelphia on August 16, 1815. Thus, the printing activities of a family that had started more than fifty years earlier ended generally unnoticed in the same city.

*   *   *

The second printing office in Delaware was established in Wilmington by Jacob Allee Killen. He was born near Dover, Delaware, a son of William Killen, first Chief Justice of Delaware under the Constitution of 1776 and first Chancellor under the Constitution of 1792. After reputedly learning the printing trade from the elder James Adams in Wilmington, he worked in Baltimore during the years of 1783 and 1784 in partnership with John Hays. From October 31, 1783, until April 9, 1784, they published the well-known *Maryland Ga-*

22. *Ibid.*, i, 47.
23. McCulloch, p. 133.

zette. After dissolving this partnership, Killen came to Wilmington later in 1784. By June of the next year he had already established a printing shop on the "west side of Market Street opposite the post-office," offering to do "all kinds of printing with accuracy and despatch."[24]

On June 14, 1785, Jacob Killen started the *Delaware Gazette* in Wilmington. After the doubtful publication of James Adams mentioned above, this is the first authenticated newspaper issued in Delaware. With some changes in title, Killen published this weekly for almost two years. He then sold it to Frederick Craig and Co., a partnership consisting of Craig, Samuel Andrews and Peter Brynberg. The new owners continued the newspaper with the issue for April 11, 1787. Jacob Killen printed in Delaware about two years. During this time he was able to secure for himself practically all the public printing. Possibly the influence of his father was instrumental in diverting the state contracts from James Adams. Except for the newspaper, he seems to have printed only a few broadsides and forms, the votes and proceedings of the House of Assembly and the session laws. Little is known about his activities after he stopped printing. He still operated a store in Wilmington in 1790, offering for sale "writing paper, spelling books, primers, wafers, blank bonds, etc., Haerlem oil, Davis golden drops, an infallible cure for the toothache . . ."[25] In 1813 Jacob Stout leased from him for six years a plantation in Duck Creek Hundred, Delaware, which was left to him by his father, William Killen.[26] The statement by

24. Advertisement in the *Delaware Gazette*, June 28, 1785.
25. *Ibid.*, May 8, 1790.
26. Lease, held by the Historical Society of Delaware, Wilmington.

Henry C. Conrad that in 1803 he published the newspaper, the *Federal Ark*, in Wilmington, is erroneous.[27]

* * *

Frederick Craig, the leading member in the partnership that took over the *Delaware Gazette* from Jacob Killen, was born about 1756. He served as a soldier in the Revolutionary War. It is not known where he learned his printing trade. The firm of Frederick Craig and Co. emerged in 1787. They began to publish the newspaper on April 11 of the same year and continued it until March, 1791, when Craig left the partnership. The business was carried on by Andrews and Brynberg. The firm of Frederick Craig and Co. was active for about five years. Its printing office was on Market Street "three doors below the Indian King." Besides publishing and printing the *Delaware Gazette*, the firm also issued more than thirty other publications which are known today. They had a substantial share of official printing, issuing some of the votes and proceedings of the House and the Senate, several of the session laws and a few other minor publications. At least two editions of the federal constitution, a collection of federal laws and several almanacs carry their imprint. Some of their publications, including the *Acts Passed at a Congress of the United States of America*, 1790, and Thomas Dilworth's *The Schoolmasters Assistant*, 1791, have the imprint Andrews, Craig and Brynberg. It is not known whether this imprint may mean a different agreement between the partners.

27. This newspaper was started at Dover in 1802 by William Black and then moved by him to Wilmington. See Clarence S. Brigham, *History and Bibliography of American Newspapers, 1690–1820* (Worcester, American Antiquarian Society, 1947), I, 83.

After Frederick Craig left the firm, he continued as a book-seller and storekeeper in Wilmington. The Banneker almanac for 1795 was printed for him by John and Samuel Adams. In 1800 he sold his store, then called the "iron-mongering busi-ness," to Samuel Spackman, who notified the public that he had moved the store from the house of Frederick Craig to a new location on Market Street.[28] In 1803 Craig was active as the keeper of the Delaware Inn in Philadelphia, inviting trav-elers, especially Delawareans, to patronize "that commodious inn . . . near the corner of Chesnut and Third Street."[29] He did not stay long in this business but returned to Delaware and spent most of his later years as the manager of the Wil-mington Almshouse. He took an active part in community life, was one of the organizers of the Wilmington Library Company and became a Justice of the Peace in October, 1825. He was remarkably active up to a very advanced age, and his mind retained its intellectual powers and a most extraordi-nary memory.[30] He died in Wilmington on July 4, 1841,[31] one of the oldest citizens of the community. He was buried at the Friends' Cemetery.

* * *

Samuel Andrews was born on June 15, 1764, in or near Wil-mington, a son of John and Sarah Andrews, a local Quaker family.[32] His name first appears in 1789 as a partner of Peter

28. *Mirror of the Times & General Advertiser*, July 12, 1800.
29. *Ibid.*, April 6, 1803.
30. Elizabeth Montgomery, *Reminiscences of Wilmington, in Familiar Village Tales* (Philadelphia, T. K. Collins, 1851), p. 74.
31. Obituary in the *Delaware Gazette*, July 9, 1841.
32. Record card of the Wilmington Society of Friends, on file at the Historical Society of Delaware, Wilmington.

Brynberg, but, according to Brigham, he was already active in 1787 as one of the partners in Frederick Craig and Co.[33] There is no evidence that he ever had his own printing business. The business relationship of Craig, Andrews, and Brynberg is not entirely clear. During the years when the firm of Frederick Craig and Co. was active, publications with the imprints "Andrews and Brynberg" or "Brynberg and Andrews" were also issued. The printing establishment of Andrews and Brynberg was located in Wilmington at the post office on Market Street. When Craig withdrew from the partnership, Andrews and Brynberg continued to work together until sometime in 1796. After that year Andrews' name does not appear on any known publication. He died in 1821 in Wilmington and was interred at the Friends' Cemetery. According to an obituary in the *American Watchman*, May 8, 1821, he was mourned by a large number of friends because "few men possessed a kinder heart or a disposition more generally useful."[34]

The name of Samuel Andrews appears on at least sixty items. This is more than one third of the titles published in Delaware during the existence of the firms with which he was connected. In addition to these, he had some responsibility for publications issued under the imprint of Frederick Craig and Co. The firm of Brynberg and Andrews had a considerable share of the official printing and was responsible for, among other publications, the printing of the minutes of the Delaware Constitutional Convention, 1791–1792. They printed various religious works, among them a New Testament,

33. Brigham, i, 81.
34. *American Watchman*, May 8, 1821.

and issued several almanacs. Schoolbooks and other educational texts including *A New Guide to the English Tongue* and *The Schoolmaster's Assistant*, both by Thomas Dilworth, and *The New American Spelling-Book* by John Peirce had a good reception. Some of them appeared in more than one edition. From the press of Brynberg and Andrews came the first catalog of the Wilmington Library Company in 1789. In 1791 they printed one of the most important books published in Delaware before 1800. This was Robert Coram's *Political Inquiries: to Which is Added, a Plan for the General Establishment of Schools Throughout the United States*. It is recognized as one of the earliest proposals for government aid to education.[35]

The printing program of Andrews and Brynberg included a variety of works. In 1792 they issued Henry Colesberry's dissertation, *Tentamen Medicum Inaugurale de Epilepsia*, and in the following year a useful book on agriculture, John Spurrier's *The Practical Farmer*. They did not, however, neglect to provide the public with lighter reading like the *History of Little Goody Two-Shoes* and Marmontel's *The Shepherdess of the Alps*.

* * *

Peter Brynberg, the third partner of the firm of Frederick Craig and Co., was a descendant of one of the early Swedish families of Delaware. Born in or near Wilmington in 1755, he later became a prosperous printer, editor, bookseller and gen-

---

35. Robert Coram was a naval veteran of the Revolutionary War, served as a schoolteacher in Wilmington and was for a short time librarian of the Wilmington Library Company. He was also the publisher of the *Delaware Gazette* from September 8, 1795, until his death on March 9, 1796. For more on him, see Charles A. Beard, *The American Spirit* (New York, Macmillan, 1942), p. 126–137.

eral merchant. By May 7, 1777, at the age of twenty-two, he had already acquired some real estate.[36] His name appears on the list of taxable persons and estates in Christiana Hundred, Delaware, in 1787.[37] He took an active part in the community life in Wilmington, being one of the first directors of the Wilmington Library Company, a member of the Friends of Justice, an assistant burgess of Wilmington several times between 1794 and 1804, and the chief burgess in 1796. He was the only printer in Delaware to be accorded this last honor.[38] Brynberg actively promoted the building of turnpike roads, particularly the Wilmington and Christiana Turnpike which was finally built in 1808. He served as a state senator from New Castle County and as a member of the Delaware House of Representatives.[39] He was married to Lydia Walraven; their daughter Ann married Robert Porter, who became a prominent Wilmington printer during the 19th century.[40]

Brynberg began his printing career in 1787 as a member of the firm of Frederick Craig and Co. After 1789 his name appears also as a partner of Samuel Andrews. They worked together until 1796 when Andrews withdrew from the business. Brynberg continued alone and was active until at least 1814. His son-in-law, Robert Porter, joined Brynberg in the business about 1812 and continued after his death.

During his many years as a printer, Peter Brynberg issued a large number of publications. His name appears on more

36. Deed, held by the Historical Society of Delaware, Wilmington.

37. John T. Scharf, *History of Delaware, 1609–1888* (Philadelphia, L. J. Richards, 1888), p. 882.

38. *Ibid.*, p. 637–8.

39. Conrad, p. 264 and 272.

40. *Delaware History*, viii, no. 3 (March, 1959), p. 203.

than one hundred and twenty works printed before 1801 and on many more until 1814. He was the second most active printer in Delaware after the elder James Adams. Among his publications was the *Delaware Gazette*, with which he was first connected as a partner in the firm of Frederick Craig and Co. Later he printed and published this paper jointly with Samuel Andrews until the beginning of September, 1795, when it was taken over by Robert Coram as publisher and editor and was printed by Bonsal & Starr. The statement that Brynberg established a magazine entitled *The Christian Repository* sometime before 1800[41] or in 1803[42] is untrue. This publication was started by Robert Porter in 1821.[43]

The production of Brynberg shows more variety than that of any other printer of this period in Delaware. Such popular publications as almanacs, religious works, collections of hymns and several primers and other schoolbooks constituted a substantial part of his work. To satisfy a demand for light reading, he printed fiction and adventure stories such as Defoe's *The Life and Most Surprising Adventures of Robinson Crusoe*. Among the more noteworthy Brynberg imprints are John Entick's *New Spelling Dictionary*, an edition of the *Arabian Nights* and the autobiography of Benjamin Franklin. Peter Brynberg died in Wilmington on July 13, 1816, and was buried at Old Swedes' Cemetery. He left a substantial estate.[44]

41. Scharf, p. 451.
42. Conrad, p. 1087, and McMurtrie, ii, 251.
43. Carroll W. Pursell, "The Fortunes of a Religious Newspaper: The Christian Repository and the Crusader, 1821–1825," *Presbyterian Historical Society Journal*, xxxviii (1960), p. 91–102.
44. Peter Brynberg's will and administration of his estate at Delaware State Archives, Dover.

*   *   *

The firm of Bonsal & Starr emerged in Wilmington in September, 1795, as the printers of the *Delaware Gazette*. This newspaper was taken over from Andrews and Brynberg by Robert Coram beginning with the issue of September 8. Coram was connected with the paper only for a short time. After his death on March 9, 1796, Bonsal & Starr printed and published the *Delaware Gazette* until it was purchased by William Catherwood Smyth on October 29, 1796.

Vincent Bonsal was born in Wilmington on April 30, 1773, as one of the seven children of Philip Bonsal, a local shopkeeper.[45] At the age of twenty-two, he and Caleb Starr, another young member of the Society of Friends, opened a printing shop on Market Street in Wilmington. Other than the *Delaware Gazette* only three items are known to have been printed by them, all in 1795. One is a religious and moral work entitled *Some Account of the Life and Religious Labours of Sarah Grubb,* the other is the *Treaty of Amity, Commerce and Navigation Between His Britannic Majesty, and the United States of America.* The third, entitled *The Universal Interpreter of Dreams and Visions,* was printed by the partners for the Baltimore bookseller, George Keatinge. The partnership probably ended when William Catherwood Smyth began to print and publish the *Delaware Gazette* in October, 1796. No evidence is available that Caleb Starr was active in the printing trade after that time. He died a rich man in Wilmington in 1851.[46]

45. Record card of the Wilmington Society of Friends, on file at the Historical Society of Delaware, Wilmington.
46. Administration of the estate of Caleb Starr at Delaware State Archives.

Bonsal continued to operate the printing shop alone for a short time. During this period he printed at least one book, *The Beauties of Hervey*, for Robert Campbell, a Philadelphia bookseller. Later in 1796, he formed a new partnership with another young printer, Hezekiah Niles. In addition to running a printing shop, they had a bookstore on Market Street in Wilmington. In 1799 they opened another bookstore in Baltimore at 173 Market Street. Their partnership continued until the end of 1804 when financial difficulties brought its dissolution. Bonsal remained in Baltimore as a bookseller and stationer in partnership with his brother, Isaac, until September, 1806, and thereafter alone. He died at Natchez, Mississippi, on July 29, 1811.[47]

Practically all publications with which Vincent Bonsal was connected as a printer or publisher were issued in partnership with Hezekiah Niles. Niles is the only Delaware printer who gained a national reputation. This was not, however, the result of his printing and publishing activities in Wilmington, but rather of his *Weekly Register* which he later printed and published in Baltimore. For this reason his life and work is relatively well known; he has the distinction of being the only Delaware printer represented in the *Dictionary of American Biography*. He was born on October 10, 1777, at Jefferis Ford, East Bradford township in Chester County, Pennsylvania. His parents were residents of Wilmington, Delaware, but at the time of his birth had sought refuge from the British at the farmhouse of their friend, James Jefferis. Hezekiah spent his childhood in Wilmington and was probably educated at the

---

47. Rollo G. Silver, *The Baltimore Book Trade, 1800–1825* (New York, New York Public Library, 1953), p. 17.

Friends' School. When he was fourteen years old, his father was accidentally killed. Three years later Hezekiah was apprenticed to Benjamin Johnson, a Philadelphia printer. From Johnson he learned both typesetting and bookbinding. While in Philadelphia, he published his first essays in local newspapers during 1794. Niles returned to Wilmington sometime during 1795. Probably later that year, he issued, in partnership with the younger James Adams the *United States Almanac* for 1796.[48] During the following year they printed another issue of the almanac. There is no evidence that these two printers issued any other publications together. In addition to the joint venture with Adams, Niles had also formed a partnership with Vincent Bonsal in 1796.

Not many publications came from the press of Bonsal and Niles during the first years of their partnership. In 1796 they printed a religious tract entitled *The Travelling Millennarian* by Molleston Correy, a Baptist minister from Kent County, Delaware, and the *Articles of the Reliance Fire Company* of Wilmington. The following year a few more religious works and *A Compendium of Practical and Experimental Farriery* by William Taplin were printed. For unknown reasons, no publications with their imprint are known for the year 1798, but during 1799 their business expanded considerably. From March 14 to September 7 they printed the *Delaware Gazette* for John Vaughan and Daniel Coleman who had taken the

48. There has been confusion about the time Niles returned to Wilmington. His biographer, Gabriel Stone, states that this happened in 1797 and that as his first work in Wilmington, he published an almanac in partnership with John Adams. Niles' partnership with Vincent Bonsal was thought to have begun in early 1799, cf. Gabriel Stone, *Hezekiah Niles as an Economist* (Baltimore, Johns Hopkins Press, 1933), p. 33–56. Some of this erroneous information has been repeated in the sketch of Niles in the *Dictionary of American Biography*.

paper over from William Catherwood Smyth. The paper was discontinued in September. It was to have been resumed by James Wilson after a short suspension. Wilson later changed his mind and established on November 20, 1799, a new paper, the *Mirror of the Times*.[49] Two other newspapers entitled the *Delaware Gazette* were published in Wilmington during the nineteenth century, but these had no connection with the *Delaware Gazette* which had been established by Jacob A. Killen in 1785, continued by a number of other publishers and finally suspended in 1799.

During the same year Bonsal and Niles issued *The Town and Country Almanac* and several textbooks including *The American Tutor's Assistant* and *A Compendious System of Practical Surveying*, both by Zachariah Jess, a Wilmington schoolteacher. Another edition of Dilworth's *The Schoolmaster's Assistant*, as well as the first book on chemistry printed in Delaware, the *Chemical Syllabus* which was a short outline by the Wilmington physician, John Vaughan, were also printed by the partners during 1799. The production of the next year included another issue of the almanac, James Davidson's *A Short Introduction to Latin Grammar* and *A Tour Through Upper and Lower Canada* by John Cosens Ogden. Another edition of Jess' *The American Tutor's Assistant*, the *Arabian Nights* and a few other volumes completed the firm's production within the period under survey. They continued their printing and publishing in Wilmington until the end of 1804 when their business failed, mainly due to losses incurred as a result of the publication of the two volume set of John Dickinson's *Political Writings* in 1801.

49. Brigham, I, 81.

During his residence in Wilmington, Hezekiah Niles was active in local political affairs. He was elected town clerk and also served as an assistant burgess several times between 1800 and 1805. In this last year in Wilmington he started his first important publication, the *Apollo, or Delaware Weekly Magazine*. It failed to create interest and was published only from February 16 to July 20, 1805.[50] In the autumn of the same year, Niles moved to Baltimore where he found an opportunity for success. Baltimore was not a strange place to him; he had owned a bookshop and stationery store there in partnership with Vincent Bonsal until September of 1804. Now he established himself as a printer, bookseller and stationer at the corner of Baltimore and Frederick Streets; later the location of his business changed several times.[51] During his first six years in Baltimore, Niles printed and published the *Baltimore Evening Post*. He sold this paper in June of 1811 to Thomas Wilson and then began publication of the *Weekly Register*. Niles soon developed this into a successful and influential periodical. In 1836 he turned over the direction of the *Register* to his son William Ogden Niles and retired. He spent his last years in Wilmington and, after having been confined to his bed for a long time by a paralytic stroke, died on April 2, 1839.

* * *

Known more as a publisher of newspapers than a printer, William Catherwood Smyth first entered business as a part-

50. Ralph R. Shaw and Richard H. Shoemaker, *American Bibliography* (New York, Scarecrow Press, 1958–1965), no. 7877.
51. Silver, p. 44–5.

ner of John and Samuel Adams. Together they published the *Delaware and Eastern-Shore Advertiser* from May 14, 1794, until March 18, 1795, when the partnership was dissolved and the Adams brothers continued alone. During their partnership Smyth and the Adams brothers issued at least two other publications, Banneker's *Wilmington Almanac* for 1795 and the *Declaration of the Political Principles of the Patriotic Society of New Castle County.*

For a short time in 1796, Smyth was involved in publishing a newspaper in Baltimore. Philip Edwards, editor and publisher of the *Maryland Journal,* took him into partnership beginning with the issue of August 2. Their joint venture was not successful and the partnership was terminated on September 8 of the same year.[52]

On September 7, 1796, Smyth purchased the *Delaware Gazette* which had been published by Bonsal and Starr after the death of its former owner, Robert Coram, earlier that year. The name of William Catherwood Smyth as printer and publisher appeared on this newspaper with the issue of October 29, and the address of the paper was given as being at the "rear of the new fire-engine, Shipley Street, opposite Capt. O'Flinn's tavern."[53] With some changes in the frequency of publication and format, he issued this newspaper until September 7, 1799. Because of a yellow fever epidemic in Wilmington, it was suspended in September and October of 1798. Under the authority of the Health Office, during these months Smyth issued a small sheet entitled the *Wilmington Mercury,*

52. Brigham, I, 241.
53. Later the address was given as "two doors below Mr. Brinton's tavern, High Street."

"printed occasionally and delivered gratis to the patrons of the Delaware Gazette."[54] In 1797 Smyth published John Dickinson's *The Letters of Fabius*, one of the most important publications of the Delaware press of the period. The first nine letters had appeared earlier in newspapers but were never before published together. There are two variants of this work. Most of the copies were issued anonymously; only one which carries the author's name on the title page is known, and it is presently held by the Wilmington Institute Free Library.

With the issue of March 14, 1799, the *Delaware Gazette* was taken over by John Vaughan and Daniel Coleman, though Smyth still continued to print it until its final suspension in September of the same year. Smyth soon began to make plans for another newspaper. On February 1, 1800, he published the first issue of the *Monitor; or Wilmington Weekly Repository*. This paper appeared weekly until June and then became a semiweekly under the title the *Monitor & Wilmington Repository*. Before it failed in the fall of 1802, it once more changed its name to the *Monitor; or, Delaware Federalist*. Misfortune with the *Monitor* did not discourage Smyth. Within the next year he was again publishing a newspaper, this time in partnership with William Black. Together they issued in Wilmington the *Federal Ark*, a paper that William Black had formerly published at Dover, Delaware. The first issue of the *Federal Ark* in Wilmington came out on February 28, 1803. The partnership of Smyth and Black had a very short life, however, and was dissolved sometime between April 13 and July 27 of that year.[55]

54. Brigham, I, 81.   55. *Ibid.*, I, 83–4.

Few other publications, all rather slim pamphlets, are known to have been printed by William Catherwood Smyth. Among the most noteworthy are John Vaughan's *Observations on Animal Electricity* and John Law's *An Inaugural Dissertation on the Rationale of the Operation of Opium on the Animal Economy*, both printed in 1797. There is no evidence that he printed in Delaware beyond the year 1803.

* * *

Joseph Johnson was active as a printer in Wilmington for a very short time. Nothing is known about his private life except that some of his descendants married into the Brynberg and Porter families.[56] In 1796 he had established himself as a printer and bookseller at "No. 73 Market Street, opposite the bank." During this year he issued at least six publications, one of them under the imprint of Joseph Johnson & Co. It is not known who his partners were, but as most of his publications during the following year carried the imprint Johnson & Preston, it is probable that Preston was already his partner in 1796. Preston has not been further identified, as information about him could not be found.[57]

About ten publications issued by Johnson are known, two of them printed in partnership with Preston. One item printed in 1800 carries the imprint "Printed by B. & J. Johnson, No. 147 High Street." No publications printed by Joseph Johnson or any of his partners are known from the years 1798 and

56. Genealogical file at the Historical Society of Delaware, Wilmington.
57. A William Preston was listed among the taxable persons and estates in Christiana Hundred, Delaware, in 1787, cf. Scharf, p. 884. He is probably the William Preston who, together with his wife, died in Wilmington of yellow fever in February, 1802. The administration of his estate is at the Delaware State Archives, Dover.

1799, nor after 1800. Judging from the known titles, Johnson was primarily a printer of religious and moral works. These include Arnauld Berquin's *The Blossoms of Morality*, and his *Children's Friend*, intended for the edification of young ladies and gentlemen. Both were popular works of the day and were also issued by several other printers outside of Delaware. Daniel Defoe's *Religious Courtship* and Christian G. Saltzmann's *Elements of Morality* are additional samples of his selection and taste. *The Contrast*, a novel by Elizabeth Sarah Villa-Real Gooch, seems to be the only non-religious work among his publications. Johnson was an exception among the Delaware printers for he did not issue a newspaper.

* * *

One of the most prominent Wilmington printers and publishers was James Wilson. He made his reputation more by editing and publishing influential newspapers than by printing books. Wilson was born on August 27, 1764, in Harford County, Maryland, of Quaker parents. In the late 1780's, he learned the printer's trade in Wilmington under Frederick Craig, who was then the printer and publisher of the *Delaware Gazette*. In 1796 he married a sister of Samuel Andrews, another Wilmington printer. His relations with the Society of Friends became strained, and he was read out of the Wilmington Monthly Meeting in October, 1796. Later in his life he was suspected of indifference toward religion. When he appeared after many years once again at a Friends' meeting, his presence created considerable astonishment.[58] Sometime in

58. *Christian Repository*, II, no. 14 (July 13, 1822), p. 56.

1796[59] he opened a printing shop and a book and stationery store in Wilmington, "at the sign of Shakespeare, at No. 5 High Street, opposite the Upper Market." He also became known as a skilled bookbinder. At first his printing program was quite limited. Only six publications issued during 1796 carry his name. Two of them have the notice "printed by J. Wilson, book-binder, bookseller and stationer." The other five items were "printed for and sold by James Wilson." It seems that Wilson had contracted other printers for these works. The books concerned represent a rather interesting selection. They include an abridgment of Henry Bracken's popular *Farriery* and Elizabeth Gooch's novel, *The Contrast.* The latter was printed by Joseph Johnson who provided the book with two different imprints, one for the copies he sold himself and the other for those he printed for James Wilson. Daniel Defoe's *Robinson Crusoe* was printed in the same year in Wilmington by Peter Brynberg who also produced the copies for Wilson with his imprint. *Letters Written During a Short Residence in Sweden, Norway, and Denmark* by Mary Wollstonecraft was printed for and sold by J. Wilson & J. Johnson, and was probably printed by the latter. The *Address of George Washington* was also printed at New Castle during 1796 by Samuel and John Adams, but the pagination and format are different and these two versions were apparently printed separately. Of Wilson's first year's production, only the *Roman Stories; or The History of the Seven Wise Masters of*

59. One of James Wilson's publications, Ralph Harrison's *Rudiments of English Grammar*, has been assigned earlier by the Library of Congress to the year of 1788, thus giving reason for the assumption that Wilson's printing career began already at that time. On the basis of an advertisement in this volume, it was, however, most likely printed in 1800.

Rome was a new publication in Delaware, and it was later reissued by Peter Brynberg in 1797.

Only one publication by Wilson from the year of 1797 is known. It is *The Syren*, containing songs then being popularized in England by Charles Dibdin, John Edwin and other performers. This was also "printed for, and sold by James Wilson." Each section of this work has a half-title with a legend: "Printed for Bonsal & Niles, and James Wilson." Again, this work was probably printed by the firm of Bonsal & Niles. No publications with Wilson's name are known for the year 1798.

A revival of Wilson's printing activity took place in 1799. He had planned to take over the *Delaware Gazette* in the autumn, but later abandoned this idea and started a new paper on November 20 entitled the *Mirror of the Times & General Advertiser*. It was a semiweekly publication and was issued with occasional irregularity until August 22, 1806. This newspaper was notable for its white paper manufactured by Thomas Gilpin in his mill on the Brandywine in Delaware.[60]

About a dozen publications, not counting the newspaper, emerged from James Wilson's printing shop during the following year. He now called his business "The Franklin Press" and, as far as is known, did not contract any work with other printers. All of these publications are of moderate size. They include three funeral orations on the death of George Washington and John J. Beckley's eight page *Epitome on the Life & Character of Thomas Jefferson*. Political activity in Delaware during the election campaign of 1800 is reflected in items like

60. McMurtrie, II, 252.

the *Address to the Citizens of Kent, on the Approaching Election.* During the year 1800 Wilson also printed a small collection of Thomas Campbell's poems, *The Pleasures of Hope,* John Vaughan's *Valedictory Lecture, Delivered Before the Philosophical Society of Delaware* and a small pamphlet in verse entitled *The Wilmingtoniad.* The last item was a reprint from the *Mirror of the Times.* According to Evans, it was written either by Wilson himself or by John Vaughan, but it has also been attributed to Joseph Bringhurst on the basis of a manuscript note on one of the copies. A few other publications such as Samuel Rogers' *The Pleasures of Memory* and Anna L. Barbaud's *Lessons for Children* completed his production for 1800. Since his printing program was not ambitious, he directed most of his energy toward publishing his newspaper[61] and involved himself in local political life. Wilson continued printing and publishing for many years, averaging about six items each year, most of which were minor publications. He disregarded the religious field almost entirely and published more political writings than any other Delaware printer of his time.

Wilson discontinued the *Mirror of the Times* with the issue of August 22, 1806. Three years later, in August 1809, he founded a new semiweekly newspaper entitled the *American Watchman; and Delaware Republican.* After publishing this paper for several years, he sold it to Selleck Osborn in 1817.[62] He continued his printing business and bookstore and was active at least until 1823.[63] James Wilson died in Wilming-

61. By the standards of the time, Wilson's paper was a strong and intelligent one, but was not making money, cf. Scharf, p. 451.

62. Brigham, I, 78.

63. Clayton D. Loughran, "A Checklist of Delaware Imprints from 1816 Through 1835." Thesis (MSLS) Catholic Univ. of America (1956), no. 124.

ton in 1841; his descendants continued his business for many years.

* * *

Except for John and Samuel Adams, William Black was the only eighteenth century Delaware printer who worked outside of Wilmington. He established a printing shop at Dover, a small town near the center of the state which had served as the capital of Delaware since 1777. Dover thus became the third Delaware town to have its own press.

Before coming to Delaware, Black had been active in New Jersey. In partnership with Gershom Craft in Trenton, he founded in July, 1798, a weekly newspaper entitled the *Federalist; or New Jersey Gazette.* The partnership lasted only for a few weeks. Black moved to Salem, New Jersey, where he started another newspaper, the *Observer*, in December of the same year, this time in partnership with Marcus North.[64] This newspaper had also a rather short life; probably only thirty-six numbers were issued. By September, 1799, William Black had established himself at Dover. Here again he started a newspaper. On September 14 he printed the first issue of the *Friend of the People.* Only one issue of this newspaper has been located, and it is not known how long it was published.

One of the reasons Black decided to move to Dover was probably his hope of securing contracts for state printing. During 1800 he was able to print only a portion of the session laws, but practically all official printing was done by him for the years of 1801 and 1802. Only three small items besides

64. Brigham, I, 516–7.

the laws printed by William Black during 1800 have survived, among them *The Mite of Praise*, a eulogy of George Washington. His production at Dover did not increase much during the following years. He started another newspaper there in September, 1802, a semiweekly entitled the *Federal Ark*. The response was poor, and he decided to transfer his operations to Wilmington. Because of the yellow fever epidemic in Wilmington in 1802, he had to postpone his move until the following year. In partnership with William Catherwood Smyth, he published the first issue of the *Federal Ark* in Wilmington on February 28, 1803. At some time between April 13 and July 27 of the same year, Smyth withdrew from the partnership and Black continued as the sole publisher. The last known issue of this paper is that of June 13, 1804. Only three other publications are known to have been published by Black in Wilmington.

In July, 1804, William Black went to Charleston, South Carolina, and was lost at sea on the return trip in September. He left behind a modest estate which just sufficed to cover his debts.[65]

*　*　*

The story of printing in Delaware during the eighteenth century is not dramatic. There were only a few printers who left behind a lasting mark of their activities. For a considerable time, just one printer was enough to satisfy the needs of the area. After the Revolution, as the population increased and the demands of the local government grew, other printers were encouraged to establish themselves in Delaware. Print-

65. Administration of the estate of William Black, at Delaware State Archives.

ing presses and type became cheaper and more available, both being made in Philadelphia after 1785. Toward the end of the century, competition among the several printers became so keen that some were constantly in financial difficulties. Not all printers could continue long in their business and many had to look for other means of livelihood; others left Delaware to seek prosperity elsewhere. Just a few printers like James Adams, Peter Brynberg and James Wilson were able to make their trade profitable in Delaware.

There are 566 known titles from the production of the several presses in Delaware during the forty years from 1761 to 1801. This figure includes the newspapers, listed once each year during which they were published, and the annual issues of almanacs. Some of these publications have not survived; there is doubt whether some others were ever printed. The list includes a variety of works. By far the largest group consists of official state publications. These include, besides the session laws and votes and proceedings of the House and the Senate, a number of proclamations and notices. They make up about one third of the total. The next largest category is religious literature, numbering some ninety separate publications. About eighty-five annual issues of different almanacs were printed during this period. These three types of publications account for more than sixty per cent of the output. The next largest group includes schoolbooks and other educational texts, numbering about forty titles. These were printed throughout the period but became more numerous during the last years of the century. Most of them were English primers, spelling books, grammars and texts of elementary mathematics. A few introductory works on surveying, bookkeeping, chemistry and geography were printed from time to time. The printing of secular works for recreational and educational reading was concentrated within the last few years of the period, and their number is almost equal to that of the textbooks. The majority of these are light, moral stories which were quite popular at the time. Only a few of these publications are of recognized literary value.

Each of the other categories includes only a handful of publications. Political writings, particularly pamphlets which were popular with many printers in other regions, were scarce in Delaware. About fifteen titles are known, most of them short tracts. Only two, Robert Coram's *Political Inquiries* and John Dickinson's *The Letters of Fabius*, were really important publications. Probably the most outstanding Delaware imprint of the period was John Filson's *The Discovery, Settlement and Present State of Kentucke*, one of only three works in the field of exploration and travel. Four works were published on agriculture and farriery, and six were devoted to different branches of science, two of them on medicine. Biography was sadly neglected; only the autobiography of Franklin can be placed in this category.

Altogether seven newspapers were published in Delaware during the eighteenth century, all except one in Wilmington. This number may be increased to nine if the doubtful titles are included. It is questionable whether the first, the *Wilmington Courant* of 1762, was ever actually printed. There is a reference to a *Dover Herald*, reputedly published at Dover in 1800, but no copy of it has been located.[66] The others in order of

66. John A. Munroe, *Federalist Delaware, 1775–1815* (New Brunswick, Rutgers Univ. Press, 1954), p. 185.

their appearance were: the *Delaware Gazette,* established in 1785 and continued through 1799; the *Delaware Courant, and Wilmington Advertiser,* issued in 1786 and 1787; the *Delaware and Eastern-Shore Advertiser,* 1794 through 1799; the *Wilmington Mercury,* printed occasionally in 1798; the *Friend of the People,* published at Dover in 1799; the *Mirror of the Times,* started in 1799 and issued until 1806; and the *Monitor; or Wilmington Weekly Repository,* published from 1800 to 1802.

The yearly production of the Delaware printers fluctuated noticeably. During the first period, from 1761 to 1784 when James Adams was the only printer, the average annual output was about six publications, ranging from three to as high as seventeen items. After other printers had established their businesses in Delaware, the average rose gradually to twenty-four publications per year, reaching from the low of thirteen items in 1786 to a peak of fifty-seven publications in 1797.

Printers in Delaware were mostly skilled craftsmen and honest and industrious workers. The running of printing presses was frequently not enough to insure sufficient income, and many printers were also bookbinders and owned book-shops and stationery stores. Their production was technically and esthetically not very different from that of fellow trades-men in Philadelphia and Baltimore. The work of James Adams is comparable to that of the best American printers of the time. Few Delaware printers promoted any particular political views, although the majority were involved in pub-lishing newspapers. James Wilson, a notable exception, was known for his political activities. Being anxious to see their business prosper, the printers tried to keep their presses busy and concentrated on publications for which there was a strong popular demand. This explains the relatively large proportion which almanacs and religious literature had in their production. The population of Delaware was small and the market for the printed word was limited. Efforts to distribute their products in the neighboring states proved unfruitful. The competition was too keen because Delaware was hedged, north and south, by important centers of printing and publishing.

The state of Delaware was not a hub of active intellectual life. Few residents were writers, and there was no appreciable supply of new works of local origin available for publication. Most of the Delaware authors, including Robert Coram, Molleston Correy, John Dickinson, Oliver Evans, James Filson, Zachariah Jess and John Vaughan, had at least some of their works printed by local printers. None of the works of the most notable Delaware poet, John Parke, were published locally, and the major work of Oliver Evans, *The Young Mill-Wright & Miller's Guide*, was printed for the author in Philadelphia.

Under these circumstances, Delaware could hardly have become a haven for printers during the eighteenth century. That so many of them still established businesses there and were, in several cases, able to build up profitable careers, is a testimony to their courage, energy and business acumen. The contributions they made to the cultural and political as well as to the business life of the community were substantial and merit recognition.

PRINTING IN DELAWARE
1761–1800

BIBLIOGRAPHICAL SOURCES

Adams: Adams, Thomas Randolph. *American Independence. The Growth of an Idea; a Bibliographical Study of the American Political Pamphlets Printed Between 1764 and 1775.* Providence, Brown University Press, 1965.

Bowker: Bowker, Richard Rogers. *State Publications; a Provisional List of the Official Publications of the Several States of the United States from Their Organization.* New York, Publishers' Weekly, 1908.

Brigham: Brigham, Clarence Saunders. *History and Bibliography of American Newspapers, 1690–1820.* Worcester, American Antiquarian Society, 1947.

Bristol: Bristol, Roger Pattrell. *Evans' American Bibliography. Supplement* (Checking ed.). Charlottesville, Bibliographical Society of the University of Virginia, 1962[–1965].

Drake: Drake, Milton. *Almanacs of the United States.* New York, Scarecrow Press, 1962.

Evans: Evans, Charles. *American Bibliography.* New York, P. Smith, 1941–1959.

Hasse: Hasse, Adelaide Rosalia. *Index to Economic Material in Documents of the States of the United States: Delaware, 1789–1904.* [Washington] Carnegie Institution of Washington, 1910.

Hawkins: Hawkins, Dorothy Lawson. "A Checklist of Delaware Imprints up to and Including 1800." Master's thesis. New York, Columbia University, 1928.

Hawkins, *Adams*: Hawkins, Dorothy Lawson. "James Adams, the First Printer of Delaware." In: *The Papers of the Bibliographical Society of America*, vol. 28, pt. 1, 1934.

Hildeburn: Hildeburn, Charles Swift Riché. *A Century of Printing. The Issues of the Press in Pennsylvania, 1685–1784.* Philadelphia [Matlack & Harvey] 1885–1886.

N.Y. Pub. Libr.: New York. Public Library. Rare Book Division. *Checklist of Additions to Evans' American Bibliography in the Rare Book Division of the New York Public Library.* Compiled by Lewis M. Stark and Maud D. Cole. New York, New York Public Library, 1960.

Reed: Reed, Henry Clay. *A Bibliography of Delaware Through 1960.* Compiled by H. Clay Reed and Marion Björnson Reed. Newark, University of Delaware Press, 1966.

Sabin: Sabin, Joseph. *Bibliotheca Americana. A Dictionary of Books Relating to America.* New York, J. Sabin [etc.] 1868–1936.

Scharf: Scharf, John Thomas. *History of Delaware, 1609–1888.* Philadelphia, C. J. Richards, 1888.

Shipton, Evans' *Early American Imprints, 1639–1800.* Clifford
microcard ed.: K. Shipton, editor. Worcester, American Antiquarian Society [1956–   ] (Reproduction on Readex microprint of the items listed in Evans' *American Bibliography*).

KEY TO LOCATIONS

CLU University of California at Los Angeles.

CSmH Henry E. Huntington Library, San Marino.

CSt Stanford University Libraries, Stanford.

CU University of California, Berkeley.

CtHT Trinity College, Hartford.

CtY Yale University, New Haven.

DAU American University Library, Washington.

DGU Georgetown University Library, Washington.

DLC U. S. Library of Congress, Washington.

DNLM U. S. National Library of Medicine, Washington.

De Delaware State Archives, Dover.

De(JD) John Dickinson's Mansion, Dover.

De(M) Delaware State Museum, Dover.

DeGE Eleutherian Mills Historical Library, Greenville.

DeHi Historical Society of Delaware, Wilmington.

DeU University of Delaware, Newark.

DeWE Episcopal Diocese of Delaware, Wilmington.

DeWF Wilmington Monthly Meeting of Friends.

DeWI Wilmington Institute Free Library.

DeWin Henry Francis du Pont Winterthur Museum, Winterthur.

ICN Newberry Library, Chicago.

IU University of Illinois, Urbana.

IaDL Luther College, Decorah.

InU Indiana University, Bloomington.

KU University of Kansas, Lawrence.

KyLx Lexington Public Library.

MB Boston Public Library.

MBAt Boston Athenaeum, Boston.

MBFM Massachusetts Grand Lodge, F. & A. M., Boston.

MCE Episcopal Theological School, Cambridge. John Gordon Wright Library.

MH Harvard University, Cambridge.

MHi Massachusetts Historical Society, Boston.

MWA American Antiquarian Society, Worcester.

MWiW Williams College, Williamstown.

MdBJ Johns Hopkins University, Baltimore.

MdBP Peabody Institute, Baltimore.

MdBS St. Mary's Seminary and University, Roland Park, Baltimore.

MdHi Maryland Historical Society, Baltimore.

MiU-C University of Michigan, Ann Arbor. William L. Clements Library.

MoHi Missouri State Historical Society, Columbia.

N New York State Library, Albany.

NBM Academy of Medicine of Brooklyn, Brooklyn.

NHi New York Historical Society, New York.

NN New York Public Library.

NNB Association of the Bar of the City of New York, New York.

NNC Columbia University, New York.

NcU University of North Carolina, Chapel Hill.

NjP Princeton University, Princeton.

NjPT Princeton Theological Seminary, Princeton.

NjR Rutgers—The State University, New Brunswick.

NjT Trenton Free Library.

OCHP Historical and Philosophical Society of Ohio, Cincinnati.

OCl Cleveland Public Library.

P Pennsylvania State Library, Harrisburg.

PAtM Muhlenberg College, Allentown.

PBL Lehigh University, Bethlehem.

PBm Bryn Mawr College, Bryn Mawr.

PCC Crozer Theological Seminary, Chester.

PCDHi Delaware County Historical Society, Chester.

PHC Haverford College, Haverford.

PHi Historical Society of Pennsylvania, Philadelphia.

PP Free Library of Philadelphia.

PPAmP American Philosophical Society, Philadelphia.

PPB Philadelphia Bar Association, Philadelphia.

PPF Franklin Institute, Philadelphia.

PPL Library Company of Philadelphia.

PPM Mercantile Library, Philadelphia (No longer in existence).

PPPD Divinity School of the Protestant Episcopal Church in Philadelphia.

PPPrHi Presbyterian Historical Society, Philadelphia.

PPRF Rosenbach Foundation, Philadelphia.

PPT Temple University, Philadelphia.

PSC Swarthmore College, Swarthmore.

PSC-Hi Swarthmore College, Swarthmore. Friends Historical Library.

PU University of Pennsylvania, Philadelphia.

PV Villanova University, Villanova.

PWcHi Chester County Historical Society, West Chester.

RPJCB John Carter Brown Library, Providence.

TxAuC Church Historical Society, Austin.

WHi State Historical Society of Wisconsin, Madison.

CHECKLIST

1. The child's new play-thing, or best amusement, being a spelling-book, intended to make the learning to read a diversion instead of a task. Consisting of Scripture-histories, fables, stories, moral and religious precepts, proverbs, songs, riddles, dialogues, &c. The whole adapted to the capacities of children, and divided into lessons of one, two, three and four syllables. Wilmington, Printed by James Adams, 1761.

Hildeburn, 1718, and the advertisement in *Pennsylvania gazette,* November 5, 1761, give title: The child's new spelling-book.

Evans 8813.
No copy known.

2. ELLIS, EVAN.
    The advice of Evan Ellis, late of Chester County, deceased, to his daughter, when at sea. Wilmington, Printed by James Adams, in his printing-office in Market-Street [1761]. § Broadside; 35 by 22 cm.

Evans 8849; Hawkins, *Adams*, p. 35.
Copies: DeHi (photocopy); DeWI (photocopy); RPJCB.

3. FOX, THOMAS.
    The Wilmington almanack, or ephemeries, for the year of our Lord, 1762 . . . Wilmington, Printed and sold by James Adams, in Market-Street [1761]. § [36] p.; 8vo.

Evans 8858.
Copies: DLC; DeWI; DeWin; MWA; PHi (now in PPL).

4. The merchants and trader's security. Wilmington, Printed by James Adams, 1761.

Evans 8928 (from adv. in *Pennsylvania gazette,* Nov. 5, 1761).
No copy known.

5. DELAWARE (COLONY) GENERAL ASSEMBLY.

Votes and proceedings of the House of Representatives of the
government of the counties of New-Castle, Kent and Sussex, upon
Delaware, at a session of Assembly held at New-Castle the twentieth day of October 1762. Published by Thomas M'Kean and Caesar
Rodney, Esquires, by order of the Assembly. Wilmington, Printed
by James Adams, in Market-Street, 1762. § 27 p.; fol.

Copies: De; MH; PHC; PHi (now in PPL).

6. DILWORTH, THOMAS, d. 1780.

A new guide to the English tongue . . . in five parts. Containing I. Words both common and proper, from one to six syllables
. . . II. A large and useful table of words, that are the same in
sound, but different in signification . . . III. A short, but comprehensive grammar of the English tongue . . . IV. An useful collection
of sentences . . . V. Forms of prayer . . . Wilmington, Printed and
sold by James Adams, 1762. § 3 p.l., 154 p.; front. (port.), illus.;
12mo.

Copies: DeWI (photocopy of title page only); NNC.

7. FOX, THOMAS.

The Wilmington almanack, or ephemeries for the year of our
Lord, 1763. Wilmington, Printed and sold by James Adams in
Market-Street [1762]. § [40] p.; 8vo.

Evans 9117.
Copies: DeWI; PHi (now in PPL).

8. [JEANNE DE LA NATIVITÉ] fl. 1650.

Daily conversation with God, exemplify'd in the holy life of
Armelle Nicolas, a poor ignorant country maid in France, commonly known by the name of Good Armelle; who departed this
life, at Bretaigne, in the year 1671. Translated from the French . . .
Wilmington, Printed by James Adams, in Market-Street, 1762.
§ 16 p.; 8vo.

Evans 9149.
Copies: PHi (now in PPL); PSC-Hi.

9.   The Wilmington courant. Wilmington, Printed and published by James Adams, 1762.

Printed for about six months? cf. Brigham, v. 1, p. 79.

Brigham; Evans 9311.
No copy known.

1763

10.   A brief instruction in the principles of the Christian religion, agreeable to the confession of faith, put forth by the elders and brethren of many congregations of Christians (baptized upon profession of their faith) in London, and in the country. To which is added, the proofs thereof, out of the Scriptures, in words at length. The seventh edition, corrected . . . Wilmington, Printed by James Adams, in Market-Street, 1763. § iv, 5–48 p.; 16mo.

Evans 9332.
Copies: PCC.

11.   DELAWARE (COLONY) LAWS.
Laws of the Government of New-Castle, Kent and Sussex, upon Delaware. Vol. I. Wilmington, Printed by James Adams, in Market-Street, 1763. § 363, xvii p.; fol.

Bristol (Evans 41337).
Copies: MdBP.

12.   DELAWARE (COLONY) LAWS.
Laws of the Government of New-Castle, Kent and Sussex, upon Delaware. Vol. II. Wilmington, Printed by James Adams, in Market-Street, 1763. § [4], iv, 81 p.; fol.

Evans 9375.
Copies: CSmH; DeHi; MdBP; NHi; NNB; PHi (now in PPL); PU.

13.   FINLEY, JAMES.
An essay on the gospel ministry wherein the nature of this ministry, the propriety of employing men therein, the importance

of it, the qualifications requisite in a gospel minister, and the means
of preserving an able and faithful ministry, and preventing its being
corrupted, are briefly considered . . . To which are added, three
addresses on the same subject. Wilmington, Printed and sold by
James Adams, 1763. § viii, 144 p.; 8vo.

Evans 9387.
Copies: DeWI; MWA; NjPT.

14. FOX, THOMAS.
The Wilmington almanack, or ephemeries for the year of our
Lord, 1764. Wilmington, Printed and sold by James Adams in
Market-Street [1763]. § [40] p.; 8vo.

Evans 9389.
Copies: DeWI; DeWin; MWA; PHi (now in PPL).

15. HOW, SAMUEL.
The sufficiency of the spirit's teaching, without humane learning: or, A treatise tending to prove humane learning to be no help
to the spiritual understanding of the word of God . . . The seventh
edition, corrected. London, Printed; and, Wilmington, Reprinted,
by James Adams, for Samuel Bond, of Cecil County, Md., 1763. §
40 p.; 8vo.

Evans 9410.
Copies: DeWI.

16. TOBLER, JOHN.
The Pennsylvania town and country-man's almanack for the
year of our Lord, 1764. Wilmington, Printed by James Adams
[1763]. § [32] p.; 8vo.

Evans 9523.
Copies: MWA (incompl.).

1764

17. DELAWARE (COLONY) LAWS.
Anno quarto Georgii III. regis. At a General Assembly begun at New-Castle, in the government of the counties of New-

Castle, Kent and Sussex, upon Delaware, the twentieth day of October, in the third year of the reign of our Sovereign Lord George the Third, King of Great-Britain, &c. annoque Domini 1763, and continued by adjournments till the thirty-first day of March following, the following acts were passed . . . [Wilmington, Printed by James Adams, 1764]. § 83–97 p.; fol.

Evans 9632.
Copies: DeHi; PPB; NNB.

18. DELAWARE (COLONY) LAWS.
Anno quinto Georgii III. regis. At a General Assembly begun at New-Castle, in the government of the counties of New-Castle, Kent and Sussex, upon Delaware, the twentieth day of October, in the fourth year of the reign of our Sovereign Lord George the Third, King of Great-Britain, &c. annoque Domini 1764, the following act was passed . . . [Wilmington, Printed by James Adams, 1764]. § 99–106 p.; fol.

Evans 9633.
Copies: DeHi; NNB; PPB.

19. ELLWOOD, THOMAS, 1639–1713.
Davideis: the life of David, King of Israel, a sacred poem. In five books . . . The seventh edition, corrected . . . London, Printed; and Wilmington, Reprinted, and sold by James Adams, at his printing office, 1764. § vi, 160, [2] p.; 12mo.

Bristol (Evans 41441); N.Y. Pub. Libr. 354.
Copies: DeWI; MWA; NN (imperfect); PHC; PWcHi.

20. FOX, THOMAS.
The Wilmington almanack, or ephemeries for the year of our Lord, 1765 . . . Wilmington, Printed and sold by James Adams in Market-Street [1764]. § [40] p.; 8vo.

Evans 9661.
Copies: DLC; DeWI; MWA; PHi (now in PPL).

21. A little looking-glass for the times, or, A brief remembrancer for Pennsylvania. Containing some serious hints, affectionately addressed to people of every rank and station in the Province:

with an appendix, by way of supplication to Almighty God. By G. C. . . . Wilmington, Printed and sold by James Adams, 1764. § v, 6–24 p.; 8vo.

Evans 9611.
Copies: DeHi (photocopy); DeWI; DeWin; NHi; PHi (now in PPL); PPRF.

22. LOCKE, JOHN, 1632–1704.
A letter concerning toleration . . . The fourth edition. Wilmington, Printed and sold by James Adams, in Market-Street, 1764. § 77 p.; 16mo.

Evans 9712.
Copies: DeHi; DeWI; MWA; PHi; PHC; PP.

23. MARKHAM, GERVASE, 1568?–1637.
The citizen and countryman's experienced farrier . . . By J. Markham, G. Jefferies and discreet Indians. London, Printed; and Wilmington, Reprinted and sold by James Adams, at his printing-office, 1764. § ix, 10–364 p.; illus.; 16mo.

Edited by John Millis, cf. Hawkins, *Adams*, p. 41.

Evans 9718.
Copies: DLC; DeHi; DeWI; DeWin; MWA; PHi (now in PPL); PPRF; PU.

24. TOBLER, JOHN.
The Pennsylvania town and countryman's almanack for the year of our Lord 1765. Wilmington, Printed by James Adams [1764].

Drake 1337; Evans 9856.
No copy known.

1765

25. ELLWOOD, THOMAS, 1639–1713.
Davideis. The life of David, King of Israel, a sacred poem. Wilmington, Printed by James Adams, 1765.

Evans 9966 (from adv. in *Pennsylvania gazette*, Apr. 18, 1765).
No copy known.

26. FOX, THOMAS.
The Wilmington almanack, or ephemeries for the year of our Lord, 1766 . . . Wilmington, Printed and sold by James Adams [1765]. § [40] p.; 8vo.

Evans 9972.
Copies: DLC; MWA; PHi (now in PPL).

27. JULIANA LIBRARY COMPANY, LANCASTER, PA.
The charter of the Juliana-Library-Company in Lancaster: and the laws of said Company. Together with a catalogue of the books, and the prices thereof, with the numbers as they stand in the library-room. The whole being collected and revised by order of the directors for this present year, 1765. By Caleb Sheward, Secretary. Wilmington, Printed by James Adams, in Market-Street, 1765. § iii, 4–47 p.; 4to.

Evans 10034.
Copies: PHi (now in PPL); PPAmP.

28. LAMBOLL, WILLIAM.
A lamentation over Zion, on the declension of the Church. By W. L., Junior. Wilmington, Printed by James Adams, 1765.

Evans 10030.
No copy known.

29. TOBLER, JOHN.
The Pennsylvania town and country-man's almanack, for the year of our Lord, 1766 . . . Wilmington, Printed by James Adams [1765].

Drake 1339; Evans 10186.
No copy known.

30. WATTS, ISAAC, 1674–1748.
Collection of hymns. By Watts, Willison and Gillis. Wilmington, Printed by James Adams, 1765.

Evans 10202 (from adv. in *Pennsylvania gazette*, Apr. 18, 1765).
No copy known.

31.   WILLISON, JOHN, 1680–1750.
The young communicant's catechism . . . Thirteenth edition. Wilmington, Printed and sold by James Adams, 1756 [i.e. 1765]. § xvii, 18–64 p.; 12mo.

Evans 10213.
Copies: DeWI.

1766

32.   DELAWARE (COLONY) LAWS.
Anno regni sexto Georgii III. regis. At a General Assembly begun at New-Castle, in the government of the counties of New-Castle, Kent and Sussex, upon Delaware, the twentieth day of October, in the sixth year of the reign of our Sovereign Lord George the Third, King of Great-Britain, &c. annoque Domini 1766, the following acts were passed . . . [Wilmington, Printed by James Adams, 1766]. § 107–123 p.; fol.

Evans 10278.
Copies: DeHi; NHi; NNB; PHi (now in PPL).

33.   FOX, THOMAS.
The Wilmington almanack, or ephemeries, for the year of our Lord, 1767 . . . Wilmington, Printed and sold by James Adams [1766]. § 40 p.; 8vo.

Evans 10299.
Copies: DeWin; MWA; PHi (now in PPL).

34.   HUME, SOPHIA, 1701–1774.
Extracts from divers antient [!] testimonies of Friends and others, corresponding with the doctrines of Christianity, recommended to the consideration, first, of ministers. Secondly, elders. Thirdly, to every member of the Church . . . [Wilmington, Printed and sold by James Adams, 1766]. § 85, [1] p.; 16mo.

Evans 10337.
Copies: DeHi; MH; PHi (now in PPL); PSC-Hi.

35. TOBLER, JOHN.
The Pennsylvania town and country-man's almanack, for the
year of our Lord, 1767 . . . Wilmington, Printed and sold by James
Adams [1766]. § [38] p.; 8vo.

Evans 10508.
Copies: CLU; DLC; MWA.

1767

36. An address to the freeholders and electors of the County of
    New-Castle, upon Delaware. By a lover of his country . . .
[Wilmington, James Adams, 1767]. § 4 p.; fol.

Signed: A freeholder of New-Castle County, and dated: Oct. 1st,
1767.

Bristol (Evans 41682); Hawkins B:2.
Copies: DeHi (not located).

37. DELAWARE (COLONY) LAWS.
    Anno regni septimo Georgii III. regis. At a General Assem-
bly begun at New-Castle, in the government of the counties of
New-Castle, Kent and Sussex, upon Delaware, the twentieth day of
October, in the seventh year of the reign of our Sovereign Lord
George the Third, King of Great-Britain, &c. annoque Domini
1767. The following acts were passed . . . [Wilmington, Printed
by James Adams, 1767]. § 125–131 p.; fol.

Evans 10600.
Copies: DeHi; NHi; NNB; PPB.

38. FOX, THOMAS.
    The Wilmington almanack, or ephemeries, for the year of
our Lord, 1768 . . . Wilmington, Printed by James Adams [1767].
§ [32] p.; 8vo.

Evans 10617.
Copies: MWA.

39. [JACOB, ELIZABETH (HEAD)] 1674–1739.
An epistle in true love, containing a farewel [!] exhortation to Friends families. Which I desire also may be read in their Monthly and Quarterly Meetings, throughout this nation of England. [Wilmington, Re-printed by James Adams in Market-Street, 1767]. § 12 p.; 8vo.

Bristol (Evans 41724); Hawkins B:3.
Copies: DeWI; PSC-Hi.

40. TOBLER, JOHN.
The Pennsylvania town and country-man's almanack, for the year of our Lord, 1768 . . . Wilmington, Printed and sold by James Adams. And to be had in Philadelphia of Jonathan Zane and William Wilson, both in Second-Street, between Chestnut and Arch-Street [1767]. § 40 p.; 8vo.

Evans 10785.
Copies: DeWI; DeWin; InU; MWA; NHi; PHi (now in PPL).

1768

41. FOX, THOMAS.
The Wilmington almanack, or ephemeris, for the year of our Lord, 1769 . . . Wilmington, Printed and sold by James Adams [1768]. § [40] p.; 8vo.

Evans 10901.
Copies: CtY; NN; NjR; PHi (now in PPL).

42. GRIFFITH, JOHN, 1713–1776.
Some brief remarks upon sundry important subjects, necessary to be understood and attended to by all professing the Christian religion. Principally addressed to the people called Quakers. London, Printed; and Wilmington, Re-printed by James Adams, 1768. § [viii], 89 p.; 8vo.

Evans 10917.
Copies: DLC; DeGE; DeHi; DeU; DeWI; DeWin; MWA; NN; PHC; PPL; PSC-Hi.

43. TOBLER, JOHN.

The Pennsylvania town and country-man's almanack, for the year of our Lord, 1769 . . . Wilmington, Printed and sold by James Adams [1768]. § [40] p.; 8vo.

Evans 11092.
Copies: DLC; DeWI; DeWin; MWA; PHi (now in PPL); PPL.

1769

44. DELAWARE (COLONY) LAWS.

Anno regni octavo Georgii III. regis. At a General Assembly begun at New-Castle, in the government of the counties of New-Castle, Kent and Sussex, upon Delaware, the twentieth day of October, in the eighth year of the reign of our Sovereign Lord George the Third, King of Great-Britain, &c. annoque Domini 1768, the following acts were passed . . . [Wilmington, Printed by James Adams, 1769]. § 133–153 p.; fol.

Evans 11235.
Copies: DeHi; NHi; NNB.

45. FOX, THOMAS.

The Wilmington almanack, or ephemeris, for the year of our Lord, 1770 . . . Wilmington, Printed and sold by James Adams [1769]. § [40] p.; 8vo.

Evans 11259.
Copies: DLC; DeWin; NjT; PHi (now in PPL).

46. TOBLER, JOHN.

The Pennsylvania town and country-man's almanack, for the year of our Lord, 1770 . . . Wilmington, Printed and sold by James Adams [1769]. § [40] p.; 8vo.

Evans 11502.
Copies: DLC; MWA; PHi (now in PPL).

47.   DELAWARE (COLONY) GENERAL ASSEMBLY.

Votes and proceedings of the House of Representatives of the government of the counties of New-Castle, Kent and Sussex, upon Delaware, at a session of Assembly held at New-Castle, the twenty-first day of October . . . 1765. Published by George Read and Thomas M'Kean, Esquires, by order of the Assembly. Wilmington, Printed and sold by James Adams, in Market-Street, 1770. § 233 p.; fol.

Includes the votes and proceedings to March 24, 1770.

Bristol (Evans 42081); Hawkins B:4.
Copies: DLC (photocopy); DeHi; PHC; PHi (now in PPL).

48.   DELAWARE (COLONY) LAWS.

Anno regni nono Georgii III. regis. At a General Assembly begun at New-Castle, in the government of the counties of New-Castle, Kent and Sussex upon Delaware, the twentieth day of October, (and continued by adjournment to the twenty-fourth day of March following) in the ninth year of the reign of our Sovereign Lord George the Third, King of Great-Britain, &c. annoque Domini 1769, the following acts were passed . . . [Wilmington, Printed by James Adams, 1770]. § 155–222 p.; fol.

Evans 11628.
Copies: DeHi; NHi; NNB; PPB.

49.   DELAWARE (COLONY) LAWS.

Anno regni decimo Georgii III. regis. At a General Assembly begun at New-Castle, in the government of the counties of New-Castle, Kent and Sussex, upon Delaware, the twentieth day of October, in the tenth year of the reign of our Sovereign Lord George the Third, King of Great-Britain, &c. annoque Domini 1770, and continued by adjournment to the third day of November following, the following act was passed . . . An act obliging persons returned and appointed for constables to serve accordingly . . . [Wilmington, Printed by James Adams, 1770]. § 223–227 p.; fol.

Evans 11629.
Copies: DLC; DeHi; NHi; NNB.

50. FOX, THOMAS.

The Wilmington almanack, or ephemeris, for the year of our Lord, 1771 . . . Wilmington, Printed and sold by James Adams [1770]. § [40] p.; 8vo.

Evans 11655.
Copies: DeWin; PHi (now in PPL).

51. TOBLER, JOHN.

The Pennsylvania town and country-man's almanack for the year of our Lord, 1771 . . . Wilmington, Printed and sold by James Adams [1770]. § [40] p.; 16mo.

Evans 11893.
Copies: DLC; DeU; InU; MB; MWA; NHi; PHi (now in PPL); PPL.

52. WALSH, THOMAS, 1730–1759.

The great salvation; and the danger of neglecting it. A sermon on Hebrews ii.3 . . . Wilmington, Printed by James Adams, 1770. § 20 p.; 4to.

Bristol (Evans 42181).
Copies: CSmH.

53. WALSH, THOMAS, 1730–1759.

The whole armour of God. A discourse delivered by the late M. Walsh, in West-Street Chapel; with an hymn on the same subject, by the Rev. Mr. Charles Wesley . . . Wilmington, Printed by James Adams, 1770. § 28 p.; 4to.

Bristol (Evans 42182).
Copies: CSmH.

54. WESLEY, CHARLES, 1707–1788.

A sermon preached on Sunday, April 4, 1742, before the University of Oxford . . . 19th ed. Wilmington, Printed by James Adams, 1770. § 12 p.; 8vo.

Bristol (Evans 42191).
Copies: CSmH.

55. The adventurers in the second class of the New-Ark land and
cash lottery, are desired to call upon the managers who signed
their respective tickets . . . [Wilmington? Printed by James
Adams? 1771]. § Broadside; 20.5 by 17 cm.

Dated above the text: Christiana Bridge, March 23, 1771.

Evans 12137; Hawkins C:1.
Copies: PPL.

56. BATES, WILLIAM, 1625–1699.
The harmony of the divine attributes, in the contrivance and
accomplishment of man's redemption by the Lord Jesus Christ . . .
London, Printed; Wilmington, Re-printed, and sold by James
Adams, in Market-Street, 1771. § iv, 501, [11] p.; 16 mo.

Evans 11978.
Copies: DLC; DeHi; DeU; DeWI; DeWin; MWA; PHi (now in
PPL); PPL; RPJCB.

57. Christiana-Bridge land & cash lottery, in New-Castle County,
on Delaware, for disposing of eight thousand, eight hundred
and seventy-six acres of land, as per scheme underneath, containing
fourty-four valuable plantations, being situated as described below,
in the province of Pennsylvania . . . Wilmington, Printed by James
Adams [1771]. § Broadside; 40 by 24 cm.

Dated above the text: December 6, 1771.

Evans 12010.
Copies: PPL.

58. Dover land and cash lottery, to be drawn in Dover, in the
County of Kent, on Delaware. For disposing of certain valuable and improved farms, and tracts of land, with stock, mills, &c.
situate on the river Saint-Croix, in the township of Newport, and
province of Nova-Scotia. [Wilmington? Printed by James Adams?
1771]. § Broadside; 46.5 by 10.5 cm.

Dated above the text: Dover, January 1, 1771.

Evans 12029; Hawkins C:2.
Copies: DLC; PPL.

59. EDWARDS, JONATHAN, 1703–1758.
The great Christian doctrine of original sin defended; evidences of its truth produced. And arguments to the contrary answered . . . [The second American edition]. Wilmington, Printed, and sold by James Adams, in Market-Street, 1771. § xv, 341 p.; 16mo.

Evans 12032.
Copies: CSmH; DeHi; DeU; DeWI; DeWin; MWA; PCC; PHi (now in PPL); PPL; PPPrHi; PSC.

60. FOX, THOMAS.
The Wilmington almanack, or ephemeris, for the year of our Lord, 1772 . . . Wilmington, Printed and sold by James Adams [1771]. § 40 p.; 8vo.

Evans 12048.
Copies: DLC; DeWI; PHi (now in PPL).

61. NELSON, JOHN, 1707–1774.
The case of John Nelson. Written by himself . . . The third edition. Wilmington, Printed by James Adams, in Market-Street, 1771. § 32 p.; 8vo.

Evans 12134.
Copies: PHi (now in PPL).

62. Newcastle lottery, instituted by the friends of the American china manufactory, for the purpose of raising the clear sum of one thousand pounds, towards the encouragement of said manufactory . . . [Wilmington? Printed by James Adams? 1771]. § Broadside; 41 by 24.5 cm.

Dated above the text: Christiana Bridge, July 13, 1771.

Evans 12140; Hawkins C:3.
Copies: PPL.

63. TOBLER, JOHN.
The Pennsylvania town and country-man's almanack for the year of our Lord, 1772 . . . Wilmington, Printed and sold by James Adams [1771]. § [40] p.; 8vo.

Evans 12248.
Copies: DLC; DeWin; MWA; PHi (now in PPL).

1772

64. DELAWARE (COLONY) LAWS.
Anno regni undecimo Georgii III. regis. At a General Assembly begun at New-Castle, in the government of the counties of
New-Castle, Kent and Sussex, upon Delaware, the twentieth day
of October, in the eleventh year of the reign of our Sovereign Lord
George the Third, King of Great-Britain, &c. annoque Domini
1771, and continued by adjournment to the thirteenth of June following, the following acts were passed . . . [Wilmington, Printed
by James Adams, 1772]. § 229–278 p.; fol.

Evans 12373.
Copies: DLC; DeHi; NHi; NNB; PPB; PPL.

65. EDWARDS, JONATHAN, 1703–1758.
The great Christian doctrine of original sin defended; evidences of its truth produced, and arguments to the contrary answered . . . Wilmington, James Adams, 1772.

Hildeburn 2767; probably same as no. 59.
No copy known.

66. FOX, THOMAS.
The Wilmington almanack, or ephemeris, for the year of our
Lord, 1773 . . . Wilmington, Printed and sold by James Adams
[1772]. § [40] p.; 8vo.

Evans 12396.
Copies: NHi; PHi (now in PPL).

67. New-Castle, February 6, 1772. Scheme of a lottery, for raising the sum . . . towards the building a Methodist preaching-
house . . . [Wilmington, Printed by James Adams, 1772]. § Broadside; 33 by 20.5 cm.

Evans 12473 (described as a Philadelphia imprint).
Copies: PPL.

76   [1772]

68. TOBLER, JOHN.
The Pennsylvania town and country-man's almanack, for the
year of our Lord, 1773 . . . Wilmington, Printed and sold by James
Adams [1772]. § [36] p.; 12mo.

Evans 12581.
Copies: InU; MWA; NHi; NN; PHi (now in PPL).

69. WATSON, THOMAS, d. 1686.
A sermon explaining the Fourth Commandment. Wilmington, Printed by James Adams for David Neilson, 1772. § 40 p.;
8vo.

Evans 12603.
Copies: PHi (now in PPL).

1773

70. DELAWARE (COLONY) GENERAL ASSEMBLY.
[Votes of the Assembly for session ending April, 1773. Wilmington, Printed by James Adams, 1773]. § 32? p.; fol.

Bristol (Evans 42433); Hawkins B:6.
Copies: DeHi (imperfect: p. 25–32 only).

71. DELAWARE (COLONY) LAWS.
Anno regni duodecimo Georgii III. regis. At a General Assembly begun at New-Castle, in the Government of the counties of
New-Castle, Kent and Sussex, upon Delaware, the twentieth day
of October (and continued by adjournments to the twelfth of April
following) in the twelfth year of the reign of our Sovereign Lord
George the Third, King of Great-Britain, &c. annoque Domini
1772, the following acts were passed . . . [Wilmington, Printed by
James Adams, 1773]. § 279–286 p.; fol.

Evans 12747.
Copies: DeHi; NHi; NNB; PHi (now in PPL); PPB.

72. DELAWARE (COLONY) LAWS.
Anno regni decimo tertio Georgii III. regis. At a General
Assembly begun at New-Castle, in the government of the counties

of New-Castle, Kent and Sussex, upon Delaware, the twentieth day of October, in the thirteenth year of the reign of our Sovereign Lord George the Third, King of Great-Britain, &c. annoque Domini 1773, the following acts were passed . . . [Wilmington, Printed by James Adams, 1773]. § 287–299 p.; fol.

Evans 12748.
Copies: DLC; DeHi; NHi; NNB; PPB.

73. A dialogue, spoken at opening the public grammar-school at Wilmington, on Tuesday, October 26, 1773. [Wilmington, Printed by James Adams, 1773]. § Broadside; 33 by 26 cm.

Evans 12750.
Copies: PPL.

74. FOX, THOMAS.
The Wilmington almanack, or ephemeris, for the year of our Lord, 1774 . . . Wilmington, Printed and sold by James Adams [1773]. § [40] p.; 8vo.

Evans 12771.
Copies: DeWI; DeWin; MdBJ.

75. TOBLER, JOHN.
The Pennsylvania town and country-man's almanack, for the year of our Lord, 1774 . . . Wilmington, Printed and sold by James Adams [1773]. § [36] p.; 8vo.

Drake 1355; Evans 13043.
Copies: DeHi; MWA.

1774

76. BOSTWICK, DAVID, 1721–1763.
A fair and rational vindication of the right of infants to the ordinance of baptism: being the substance of several discourses from Acts ii.39 . . . Wilmington, Printed and sold by James Adams in High-Street, 1774. § 54, [2] p.; 8vo.

78

Evans 13166.
Copies: MWA; PHi (now in PPL); PPPrHi.

77. DELAWARE (COLONY) GENERAL ASSEMBLY.
Votes and proceedings of the House of Representatives of the
government of the counties of New-Castle, Kent and Sussex on
Delaware. In General Assembly met at New-Castle, on Wednes-
day, October 20, 1773. Wilmington, Printed and sold by James
Adams, in High-Street, 1774. § 46 p.; fol.

Bristol (Evans 42583); Hawkins B:7.
Copies: DLC; De (photocopy); PHi (now in PPL).

78. FOX, THOMAS.
The Wilmington almanack, or ephemeris . . . for the year of
our Lord, 1775 . . . Wilmington, Printed and sold by James Adams
[1774].

Drake 1358; Evans 13281.
No copy known.

79. Know all men by these presents, that——held and firmly
bound unto——in the sum of lawful money——to be paid to
the said——. Dated the——day of——in the year of our Lord one
thousand seven hundred and . . . Wilmington, Printed and sold by
James Adams [1774?]. § Broadside; 32 by 20 cm.

Forms, filled in and dated in ink: Oct. 14, 1774; another copy dated:
August 1, 1775.

Hawkins C:4.
Copies: DeHi.

80. Know all men by these presents, that——held and firmly
bound unto John Head, of the city of Philadelphia, and province of Pennsylvania, merchant, in the sum of——. Dated the——
day of——in the year of our Lord one thousand seven hundred and
——and in the year of the reign of our Sovereign Lord . . . Wilmington, Printed by James Adams, 1774. § Broadside; 31 by 19.5
cm.

Bristol, p. 226; Hawkins C:5.
Copies: DeHi.

81. NEW CASTLE CO., DEL.
County of New-Castle on Delaware, ss. By the tenor of these presents, I——Esq.; Register for the probate of wills, and granting letters of administration for the County of New-Castle, upon Delaware——. Do make known, unto all men on the date hereof at New-Castle in the County of New-Castle aforesaid, before me was proved, approved and insinuated the last will and testament of—— [Wilmington, Printed by James Adams, 1774?]. § Broadside; 31 by 21 cm.

Form, filled in and dated in ink: Tenth day of October, one thousand seven hundred and seventy four.

Copies: DeHi.

82. [PRIESTLEY, JOSEPH] 1733–1804.
An address to Protestant dissenters of all denominations, on the approaching election of members of Parliament, with respect to the state of public liberty in general, and of American affairs in particular. [Wilmington, Printed by James Adams, 1774]. § 8vo.

Adams 131d; Evans 13557 (from adv. in *Pennsylvania packet*, Sept. 26, 1774).
No copy known.

83. To the gentlemen, freeholders and others in the County of New Castle, upon Delaware, who have a vote in the election of representatives in General Assembly. [Wilmington, James Adams, 1774]. § Broadside?

Hawkins C:6; Scharf, I:216.
No copy known.

84. TOBLER, JOHN.
The Pennsylvania town and country-man's almanack, for the year of our Lord, 1775. Wilmington, Printed and sold by James Adams [1774]. § [40] p.; 8vo.

Drake 1357; Evans 13685.
Copies: DeWin.

85. [ALLEN, JOHN] fl. 1764.
An oration, upon the beauties of liberty, or The essential rights of the Americans. Delivered at the Second Baptist-Church in Boston . . . Wilmington, Printed and sold by James Adams in High-Street, 1775. § xi, 12–21 p.; 8vo.

Attributed also to Isaac Skillman.

Adams 91g; Evans 14457.
Copies: NN; RPJCB.

86. BYRNES, DANIEL.
The following address was intended to have been published before the twentieth of the last month, but as it was omitted, it is hoped that the good end intended may not be altogether lost by its being now printed. Eighth month 4th. A short address to the English colonies, in North America . . . Wilmington, Sixth month 20th, 1775. [Wilmington, Printed by James Adams, 1775]. § [2] p.; fol.

Evans 13859.
Copies: DLC; DeU; DeWin; PHC; PHi (now in PPL); PSC-Hi.

87. DELAWARE (COLONY) COUNCIL OF SAFETY.
In Council. The Council of Safety of the counties of New-Castle, Kent and Sussex, on Delaware to——. We, reposing especial trust and confidence in your patriotism, valour, conduct and fidelity, do by these presents constitute and appoint you to be . . . [Wilmington, Printed by James Adams, 1775?]. § Broadside; 25 by 36 cm.

Form, filled in and dated in ink: 15th September, 1775.

Copies: DeHi.

88. DELAWARE (COLONY) GENERAL ASSEMBLY.
Votes and proceedings of the House of Representatives of the government of the counties of New-Castle, Kent and Sussex, on Delaware, in General Assembly met at New-Castle, from October sessions 1774 'till the end of August sessions 1775. Wilmington,

Printed and sold by James Adams, in High-Street, 1775. § 74+ p.; fol.

Copies: De (photocopy); PHi (now in PPL; imperfect: all after p. 74 wanting).

89. DELAWARE (COLONY) LAWS.
Anno regni decimo quarto Georgii III. regis. At a General Assembly begun at New-Castle, in the government of the counties of New-Castle, Kent and Sussex, upon Delaware, the twentieth day of October, in the fourteenth year of the reign of our Sovereign Lord George the Third, King of Great-Britain, &c. annoque Domini 1774, (and continued by adjournments to the twenty-first of August following), the following acts were passed . . . [Wilmington, Printed by James Adams, 1775]. § 301–351 p.; fol.

Evans 14005.
Copies: DLC; NHi; NNB.

90. DELAWARE (COLONY) LAWS.
Anno regni decimo quinto Georgii III. regis. At a General Assembly begun at New-Castle, in the government of the counties of New-Castle, Kent and Sussex, upon Delaware, the twentieth day of October in the fifteenth year of the reign of our Sovereign Lord George the Third, King of Great-Britain, &c. anoque [!] Domini 1775, the following act was passed . . . [Wilmington, Printed by James Adams, 1775]. § 353–355, 336–337 [i.e. 356–357] p.; fol.

Evans 14006.
Copies: DLC; NHi; NNB.

91. A descant on the command, Mat. xxviii.19, 20 . . . By a well-wisher to truth . . . Wilmington, Printed by James Adams, for the author, 1775. § 31 p.; 4to.

Bristol (Evans 42804).
Copies: MWA.

92. FOX, THOMAS.
The Wilmington almanack, or ephemeris for the year of our Lord 1776 . . . Wilmington, Printed and sold by James Adams [1775]. § [40] p.; 8vo.

Evans 14037.
Copies: DeWI.

93. [HARVEY, EDWARD]
The manual exercise, as ordered by His Majesty, in 1764. Together with plans and explanations, of the method generally practic'd at reviews and field-days, &c. Wilmington, Printed by James Adams, at his printing-office in High-Street, 1775. § 37 p.; 8vo.

Evans 14109.
Copies: DeHi (photocopy); DeWI; NHi; PHi (now in PPL).

94. SMITH, WILLIAM, 1727–1803.
A sermon on the present situation of American affairs. Preached in Christ-Church, June 23, 1775. At the request of the officers of the Third Battalion of the city of Philadelphia and district of Southwark . . . Wilmington, Printed and sold by James Adams, in High-Street, 1775. § iv, 5–17 p.; 8vo.

Adams 196c; Evans 14460.
Copies: PHi (now in PPL).

95. TOBLER, JOHN.
The Pennsylvania town and country-man's almanack, for the year of our Lord 1776 . . . Wilmington, Printed and sold by James Adams [1775]. § [40] p.; 8vo.

Evans 14521.
Copies: DeHi; DeWI; DeWin.

1776

96. DELAWARE. CONSTITUTIONAL CONVENTION, 1776.
In convention, at New-Castle, for the Delaware State, begun the 27th day of August, 1776, and continued by adjournment to the 21st day of September following . . . [A declaration of rights and fundamental rules of the Delaware State, formerly stiled the Government of the Counties of New-Castle, Kent and Sussex, upon

Delaware. Also the Constitution or system of government . . .
Wilmington, Printed by James Adams, 1776]. § 11 p.; fol.

Extract from the Proceedings. Attest. James Booth, Clk.

Evans 14732.
Copies: DLC; DeHi; PPL.

97.   DELAWARE. CONSTITUTIONAL CONVENTION, 1776.
Proceedings of the Convention of the Delaware State, held at
New-Castle on Tuesday, the twenty-seventh of August, 1776. Wil-
mington, Printed by James Adams, 1776. § 35 p.; fol.

Bristol (Evans 43018); N.Y. Pub. Libr., 602.
Copies: DLC; DeHi; DeWin; NN; NNB; NjP.

98.   DELAWARE. GENERAL ASSEMBLY.
In Assembly. The representatives of the freemen of the counties of New-Castle, Kent and Sussex, upon Delaware to———. We,
reposing especial trust and confidence in your patriotism, valour,
conduct and fidelity, do by these presents constitute and appoint
you to be . . . [Wilmington, Printed by James Adams, 1776?].

Form, filled in and dated: July the 27th 1776.

Copies: DeHi.

99.   DELAWARE. GENERAL ASSEMBLY.
[Paper money: four, five, six, and ten shilling notes, issued
by the General Assembly of Delaware in 1776. Wilmington]
Printed by James Adams, 1776.

Copies: DeWI.

100.   DELAWARE. GOVERNOR.
By His Excellency Caesar Rodney, Esq; President, Captain-
General and Commander in Chief of the Delaware State. A procla-
mation [of an Act to prohibit the export of provisions from the
State beyond the sea. Wilmington, Printed by James Adams,
1776]. § Broadside.

Evans 14731.
No copy known.

101. DELAWARE. LAWS.
Anno Domini millesimo septingentesimo septuagesimo sexto. Articles and rules for encouraging the association, and the better governing the militia, in the government of the counties of New-Castle, Kent and Sussex, upon Delaware. Wilmington, Printed by James Adams, 1776. § 20 p.; 8vo.

Copies: DeHi (photocopy); DeWI.

102. DELAWARE. LAWS.
Anno millesimo septingentesimo septuagesimo sexto. An act for establishing a militia in this State. Wilmington, Printed by James Adams, 1776. § 26+ p.; 12mo.

Evans 14733.
Copies: PPL (incomplete: all after p. 26 wanting).

103. FOX, THOMAS.
The Wilmington almanack, or ephemeris, for the year of our Lord, 1777 . . . Wilmington, Printed and sold by James Adams [1776]. § 40 p.; 8vo.

Evans 14760.
Copies: DLC; DeWin.

104. TOBLER, JOHN.
The Pennsylvania town and country-man's almanack for the year of our Lord 1777 . . . Wilmington, Printed and sold by James Adams [1776]. § [40] p.; 8vo.

Drake 1361; Evans 15116.
Copies: DLC; DeHi; PHi (now in PPL).

105. U.S. CONTINENTAL CONGRESS, 1775.
Journal of the proceedings of the Congress, held at Philadelphia, May 10, 1775. Wilmington, Printed and sold by James Adams, in High-Street, 1776. § 110 p.; 8vo.

Evans 15144.
Copies: DeWI; MH.

106. DELAWARE. GENERAL ASSEMBLY.
[Paper money: three, four, six, and nine pence notes, issued by the General Assembly of Delaware in 1777. Wilmington] Printed by James Adams, 1777.

Copies: DeWI.

107. DELAWARE. GENERAL ASSEMBLY. HOUSE.
Votes of the House of Assembly of the Delaware State, held at New-Castle on Monday, October 28, 1776. Wilmington, Printed and sold by James Adams, in High-Street, 1777. § 155 p.; fol.

Contains the votes from October 28, 1776 to June 7, 1777.

Copies: De (imperfect: title page and p. 3–4 in photocopy); PHi (now in PPL; imperfect: title page wanting).

108. DELAWARE. LAWS.
Anno millesimo septingentesimo septuagesimo sexto, at a General Assembly begun at New-Castle, in the Delaware State, the twenty-eighth day of October, anno Domini 1776, and continued by adjournment to the twenty-second day of February 1777, the following acts were passed. [Wilmington, Printed by James Adams, 1777]. § 339–369 p. [i.e. 359–389 p.]; fol.

Bristol (Evans 43241); Hawkins B:9.
Copies: DLC; DeWin; MdBP; NNB; PPAmP; PPL.

109. FOX, THOMAS.
The Wilmington almanack, or ephemeris, for the year of our Lord 1778 ... Wilmington, Printed and sold by James Adams [1777].

When the British occupied Wilmington in 1777, Adams moved his family and printing equipment to the neighborhood of Doylestown, Pennsylvania. He is supposed to have printed there an almanac, which was probably Fox's almanac for 1778.

Evans 15297.
No copy known.

110. DELAWARE. GOVERNOR.
By His Excellency Caesar Rodney, Esq., President, Captain-General and Commander in Chief of the Delaware State, a proclamation [appointing Wednesday the 30th of December as a day of public thanksgiving] . . . Wilmington, Printed by James Adams [1778]. § Broadside; 34 by 20.5 cm.

Dated: Dover, December 7, 1778.

Bristol (Evans 43447); Hawkins C:8.
Copies: DLC; DeHi.

111. DELAWARE. GOVERNOR.
The Delaware State to——. Know you that——President, Captain-General and Commander in Chief of the said State—— doth constitute and appoint you to be . . . [Wilmington, Printed by James Adams, 1778?]. § Broadside; 21 by 33 cm.

Form, filled in and dated in ink: 1 day of September, 1778.

Copies: DeHi.

112. DELAWARE. LAWS.
An act [of confiscation]. Wilmington, Printed by James Adams, 1778. § 6 p.; 8vo.

Evans 15780.
No copy known.

113. DELAWARE. LAWS.
Anno millesimo septingentesimo septuagesimo octavo. At a General Assembly begun at Dover, in the Delaware State, the first day of December, anno Domini 1777, and continued by adjournment till the 4th of April 1778, the following act was passed; that is to say: An act against desertion, and harbouring deserters . . . [Wilmington, Printed by James Adams, 1778]. § 4 p.; fol.

Bristol (Evans 43445); Hawkins B:10.
Copies: DLC; MiU-C; NNB; PPL.

114. DELAWARE. LAWS.
Anno millesimo septingentesimo septuagesimo octavo. At a General Assembly, begun at Dover, in the Delaware State, the first day of December, anno Domini 1777, and continued by adjournment till the 26th of June 1778, the following acts were passed; that is to say: An act for regulating and establishing the fees of divers civil officers. [Wilmington, Printed by James Adams, 1778]. § 5 p.; fol.

Bristol (Evans 43440); Hawkins B:11.
Copies: DLC; DeWin; NNB; PPL.

115. DELAWARE. LAWS.
Anno millesimo septingentesimo septuagesimo octavo. At a General Assembly begun at Dover, in the Delaware State, the first day of December 1777, and continued by adjournment till the 26th of June 1778, the following act was passed, that is to say: An act of free pardon and oblivion . . . [Wilmington, Printed by James Adams, 1778]. § 8 p.; fol.

Bristol (Evans 43442); Hawkins B:12.
Copies: DLC; DeWin; MiU-C; NNB; PPL.

116. DELAWARE. LAWS.
Anno millesimo septingentesimo septuagesimo octavo. Rules and articles, for the better regulating of the militia of this State, whilst under arms or embodied. [Wilmington, Printed by James Adams, 1778]. § 4 p.; fol.

Law passed May 15, 1778.

Copies: PPL.

117. FOX, THOMAS.
The Wilmington almanack, or ephemeris, for the year of our Lord, 1779 . . . Wilmington, Printed and sold by James Adams [1778]. § [40] p.; 8vo.

Evans 15797.
Copies: DLC; DeWI; DeWin; PHi (now in PPL).

118. NEW CASTLE CO., DEL.
New-Castle County, ss. In August session, 1778. Ordered by the Court, that the keepers of public houses within this county shall receive for the following liquors and other articles the prices herein after mentioned . . . Wilmington, Printed by James Adams [1778]. § Broadside; 21 by 17 cm.

Bristol (Evans 43517); Hawkins C:7.
Copies: De (unlocated).

119. TOBLER, JOHN.
The Pennsylvania town and country-man's almanack, for the year of our Lord 1779. Wilmington, Printed and sold by James Adams [1778]. § [46] p.; 8vo.

Copies: DeHi.

1779

120. DELAWARE. GOVERNOR.
By His Excellency Caesar Rodney, Esq., President . . . of the Delaware State, a proclamation [appointing Thursday, the sixth day of May next as a day of fasting, humiliation, and prayer throughout the state]. Wilmington, Printed by James Adams [1779]. § Broadside; 34 by 21 cm.

Dated: March 30, 1779.

Bristol (Evans 43623); Hawkins C:11.
Copies: DLC.

121. DELAWARE. GOVERNOR.
By His Excellency Caesar Rodney, Esq., President . . . of the Delaware State, a proclamation [prohibiting export of bread-stuffs, meats, etc. to any port or place in British lands, for thirty days]. Newcastle, August 31, 1779. Wilmington, Printed by James Adams [1779]. § Broadside; 35 by 21 cm.

Evans 16257.
Copies: DLC.

122. DELAWARE. GOVERNOR.

By His Excellency Caesar Rodney, Esq., President . . . of the Delaware State, a proclamation . . . to permit the exportation of . . . flour and grain . . . for . . . the State of Massachusett's Bay . . . Dover, My [!] 3, 1779. Wilmington, Printed by James Adams [1779]. § Broadside; 35 by 21 cm.

Bristol (Evans 43622); Hawkins C:10.
Copies: DLC; DeHi; DeWI; MWA; PHi.

123. DELAWARE. LAWS.

Acts of the General Assembly of the Delaware State. At a session begun at Dover on the twentieth day of October, 1778, and continued by adjournments [to May 1779]. Being their third session. Wilmington, Printed by James Adams, 1779. § 53 p.; fol.

Evans 16256.
Copies: DLC; DeWin; MdBP; NNB; PPAmP; PPL.

124. DELAWARE. SUPREME COURT.

Delaware State, ss. Samuel Patterson, of New-Castle, in the Delaware State aforesaid, Esq.: Brigadier General of Militia, came before me . . . David Kinney Esq., one of the justices of the Supreme Court, for said State and being duly sworn . . . explains how public funds in his care happened to fall into the hands of the British. [Wilmington, Printed by James Adams, 1779]. § 4 p.; fol.

Bristol, p. 280; Hawkins B:13; Heartman 661.
No copy known.

125. FOX, THOMAS.

The Wilmington almanack, or ephemeris, for the year of our Lord 1780 . . . Wilmington, Printed and sold by James Adams [1779]. § [32] p.; 8vo.

Evans 16278.
Copies: DLC; DeHi; DeWI.

126. U.S. CONTINENTAL CONGRESS, 1779.

In Congress, Friday, June 11, 1779. Resolved, that twenty million dollars . . . be borrowed on the faith of the United States of

America, at an interest of six per cent. per annum. Notice is hereby given, that in pursuance of the above resolutions of Congress the following . . . are duly authorized . . . by . . . the Delaware State to receive subscriptions . . . Wilmington, Printed by James Adams [1779]. § Broadside; 33 by 21 cm.

Signed: James Booth, Secretary.

Bristol (Evans 43715); Hawkins C:9.
Copies: DLC.

127. WADE, FRANCIS.
Advertisement. To the inhabitants of the Delaware State [concerning horse thieves, deserters, and George Evans' illegal sale of public flour. Dated Sept. 25, 1779. Wilmington, Printed by James Adams, 1779]. § Broadside; 38.5 by 24.5 cm.

Copies: DeHi.

1780

128. DELAWARE. GENERAL ASSEMBLY. HOUSE.
Votes of the House of Assembly of the Delaware State, held at Dover, on Wednesday, October 20, 1779 [to June 21, 1780]. Wilmington, Printed by James Adams, in High-Street, 1780. § 149 p.; fol.

Copies: De; PHi (now in PPL; imperfect: title page wanting).

129. DELAWARE. GOVERNOR.
President, Captain-General and Commander in Chief of the Delaware State. Whereas hath been recommended unto me, as a sober and fit person, to keep a house of public entertainment . . . [Wilmington, Printed by James Adams, 1780?]. § Broadside; 21 by 32 cm.

Form, autographed by Caesar Rodney.

Copies: PU.

130. DELAWARE. LAWS.
Acts of the General Assembly of the Delaware State, at a session begun at Dover on the twentieth day of October 1779, and

continued by adjournments; being their fourth session. Wilmington, Printed by James Adams, 1780. § 67 p.; fol.

Bristol (Evans 43793); Hawkins B:14.
Copies: DeWin; MdBP; NNB; PPL.

131. DELAWARE. LAWS.
Anno millesimo septingentesimo octuagesimo. At a General Assembly begun at Dover, in the Delaware State, the twentieth day of October, anno Domini 1779, and continued by adjournments till the twenty-ninth day of March 1780, the following acts were passed . . . [Wilmington, Printed by James Adams, 1780]. § 21–35 p.; fol.

Evans 16757; also included in no. 130.
Copies: DLC; DeWin; MdBP; NNP; PHi (now in PPL); PPL.

132. DELAWARE. LAWS.
Anno millesimo septingentesimo octuagesimo. At a General Assembly begun at Dover, in the Delaware State, the twentieth day of October, anno Domini 1779, and continued by adjournments till the eighth day of June 1780, the following acts were passed . . . [Wilmington, Printed by James Adams, 1780]. § 37–67 p.; fol.

Evans 16758; also included in no. 130.
Copies: DLC; DeWin; MdBP; NNB; PHi (now in PPL); PPL.

133. FOX, THOMAS.
The Wilmington almanack, or ephemeris, for the year of our Lord 1781 . . . Wilmington, Printed and sold by James Adams [1780]. § [32] p.; 8vo.

Evans 16778.
Copies: DeHi; DeWI; MWA; P.

1781

134. BIBLE. N.T.
The New Testament of our Lord and Saviour Jesus Christ, newly translated out of the original Greek; and with the former translations diligently compared and revised. Appointed to be read

in Churches. Wilmington, Printed and sold by James Adams, 1781.
§ 408 p.; 12mo.

Evans 17102.
Copies: DeWI; PPRF.

135. DELAWARE. GOVERNOR.
By the President of the Delaware State, a proclamation. As it is undoubtedly pleasing in the sight of Almighty God, that His rational creatures should yield a cheerful submission to His holy laws . . . exhorting all persons decently and reverently to attend the worship of God on every Lord's day . . . put into execution an act of Assembly entitled, "An act against drunkenness, and to prevent the grievous sins of profane cursing, swearing, and blasphemy," and also "An act to prevent the breach of the Lord's day, commonly called Sunday" . . . Given under my hand and the Great Seal of the State, at New Castle, this nineteenth day of November, in the year of our Lord one thousand seven hundred and eighty-one. John Dickinson, President. Wilmington, Printed by James Adams [1781]. § Broadside; 33 by 21 cm.

Evans 17134.
Copies: DLC; NN.

136. DELAWARE. GOVERNOR.
By the President of the Delaware State, a proclamation. Whereas it is discovered that the British prisoners lately captured in the State of Virginia, find means to escape from the places of their confinement . . . it is hereby enjoined and required, that all magistrates . . . be very diligent and careful . . . Given at New-Castle, this twentieth day of November, in the year of our Lord one thousand seven hundred and eighty-one. John Dickinson, President. [Wilmington, Printed by James Adams, 1781]. § Broadside; 33 by 21 cm.

Evans 17135.
Copies: NN; PPL.

137. DELAWARE. LAWS.
Acts of the General Assembly of the Delaware State, at a session begun at Dover, on the twentieth day of October 1780, and

continued by adjournments [till the twenty-eighth day of May 1781] being their fifth session. Wilmington, Printed by James Adams, 1781. § 55 p.; fol.

Evans 17133.
Copies: DLC; PPAmP; PPL.

138. DELAWARE. LAWS.
Anno millesimo septingentesimo octuagesimo primo. At a General Assembly begun at Dover, in the Delaware State, the twentieth day of October, anno Domini 1780, and continued by adjournment till the fourth day of January 1781, the following act was passed, that is to say: An act to recruit the regiment of this State ... [Wilmington, Printed by James Adams, 1781]. § 3–10 p.; fol.

Also included in no. 137.

Copies: DLC; PPL.

139. DELAWARE. LAWS.
Anno millesimo septingentesimo octuagesimo primo. At a General Assembly begun at Dover, in the Delaware State, the twentieth day of October, anno Domini 1780, and continued by adjournments till the fourth day of January 1781, the following acts were passed ... [Wilmington, Printed by James Adams, 1781]. § 11–30 p.; fol.

Also included in no. 137.

Copies: DLC; DeHi; PPL.

140. DELAWARE. LAWS.
Anno millesimo septingentesimo octuagesimo primo. At a General Assembly begun at Dover, in the Delaware State, the twentieth day of October, anno Domini 1780, and continued by adjournments till the fourth day of January 1781, the following acts were passed ... [Wilmington, Printed by James Adams, 1781]. § 31–36 p.; fol.

Also included in no. 137.

Copies: DLC; DeHi; PPL.

141. DELAWARE. LAWS.

Anno millesimo septingentesimo octuagesimo primo. At a General Assembly begun at Dover, in the Delaware State, the twentieth day of October, anno Domini 1780, and continued by adjournments till the twenty-eighth day of May 1781, the following acts were passed . . . [Wilmington, Printed by James Adams, 1781]. § 37–55 p.; fol.

Also included in no. 137.

Copies: DLC; NNB; PPL.

142. FOX, THOMAS.

The Wilmington almanack, or ephemeris, for the year of our Lord 1782 . . . Wilmington, Printed and sold by James Adams [1781]. § 40 p.; 8vo.

Evans 17157.
Copies: DLC; DeHi; DeWI; PHi (now in PPL); WHi.

143. A mournful lamentation on the untimely death of paper money: a native of North-America, who died . . . in . . . 1781 . . . [Wilmington?] Printed by Sam. Adams, in the 10th year of his age, and 1st month of his apprenticeship, 1781. § Broadside.

N.Y. Pub. Libr., 748, assigns it to a Boston printer, but no Sam. Adams is known as a printer at Boston before 1800.

Copies: NN (photocopy; location of the original unknown).

1782

144. DELAWARE. GOVERNOR.

By the President of the Delaware State, a proclamation [concerning the capture and confinement of prisoners of war] . . . Given . . . at New-Castle, the nineteenth day of April, in the year of our Lord one thousand seven hundred and eighty-two. John Dickinson. [Wilmington, Printed by James Adams, 1782]. § Broadside; 33 by 20.5 cm.

Bristol (Evans 44195).
Copies: PPL.

145. DELAWARE. GOVERNOR.

By the President of the Delaware State. A proclamation. Whereas the enemy having renounced the hope of accomplishing their designs against the United States by force alone . . . Given at New-Castle, the ninth day of July, 1782. John Dickinson, President. [Wilmington, Printed by James Adams, 1782]. § Broadside; 33 by 21 cm.

Evans 17517.
Copies: NN.

146. DELAWARE. GOVERNOR.

By the President of the Delaware State. A proclamation. Whereas the southern post was robbed of his mail, on Sunday the sixteenth day of June last, within five miles of Hartford, in the state of Maryland . . . Given . . . at New-Castle, the fifth day of July, in the year of our Lord one thousand seven hundred and eighty-two. John Dickinson. [Wilmington, Printed by James Adams, 1782]. § Broadside; 33 by 21 cm.

Evans 17516.
Copies: DLC.

147. DELAWARE. GOVERNOR.

By the President of the Delaware State. A proclamation. Whereas the United States in Congress assembled, taking into their consideration the many instances of divine goodness to these States . . . I do therefore . . . proclaim, that Thursday, the twenty-eighth day of November next, be observed throughout this State as a day of solemn thanksgiving. Given . . . at New-Castle, the thirty-first day of October, in the year of our Lord one thousand seven hundred and eighty-two. John Dickinson. [Wilmington, Printed by James Adams, 1782]. § Broadside; 33 by 21 cm.

Evans 17518.
Copies: NN.

148. DELAWARE. LAWS.

An act for inflicting penalties . . . [Wilmington, Printed by James Adams, 1782]. § 8 p.; fol.

Bristol (Evans 44191).
Copies: DLC.

149. DELAWARE. LAWS.
. . . An act to remedy defects that have arisen in the execution of an act . . . for embodying a number of militia . . . [Wilmington, Printed by James Adams, 1782]. § 6 p.; fol.

Bristol (Evans 44193).
Copies: PPL.

150. DELAWARE. LAWS.
Acts of the General Assembly of the Delaware State, at a session begun at Dover on the twentieth day of October 1781, and continued by adjournments: being their sixth session. Wilmington, Printed by James Adams, 1782. § 22 p.; fol.

Evans 17512.
Copies: MdBP; NNB; PHi (now in PPL); PPL.

151. DELAWARE. LAWS.
Anno millesimo septingentesimo octuagesimo primo. At a General Assembly begun at Dover, in the Delaware State, the twentieth day of October, anno Domini 1781, and continued by adjournment till the thirteenth day of November, the following acts were passed; that is to say: An act for raising twenty-three thousand six hundred and twenty-five pounds . . . [Wilmington, Printed by James Adams, 1782]. § 3–15 p.; fol.

Also included in no. 150.

Copies: MdBP; NNP; PHi; PPL.

152. DELAWARE. LAWS.
Anno millesimo septingentesimo octuagesimo primo. At a General Assembly begun at Dover, in the Delaware State, the twentieth day of October, anno Domini 1781, and continued by adjournment till the thirteenth day of November, the following acts were passed, that is to say: An act to vest in the Congress of the United States a power to levy duties . . . [Wilmington, Printed by James Adams, 1782]. § 17–22 p.; fol.

Also included in no. 150.

Bristol (Evans 44194); Hawkins B:15.
Copies: MdBP; NNB; PHi; PPL.

153. DELAWARE. LAWS.

Anno millesimo septingentesimo octogesimo secundo. An act for aiding and more effectually carrying into execution acts of Congress of the twentieth and twenty-seventh days of February last past. [Wilmington, Printed by James Adams, 1782]. § 6 p.; fol.

Evans 17515.
Copies: NNB; PPL.

154. DELAWARE. LAWS.

Anno millesimo septingentesimo octogesimo secundo. An act for ascertaining the depreciation of the pay-accounts of divers persons in the several departments of the Army . . . [Wilmington, Printed by James Adams, 1782]. § 4 p.; fol.

Evans 17513.
Copies: DLC; NNB; PPL.

155. DELAWARE. LAWS.

Anno millesimo septingentesimo octogesimo secundo. An act for establishing a militia within this State. [Wilmington, Printed by James Adams, 1782]. § 16 p.; fol.

Passed February 5, 1782.

Evans 17514.
Copies: DLC; NNB; PPL.

156. DELAWARE. LAWS.

Anno millesimo septingentesimo octogesimo secundo. An act for increasing the powers of the justices of the Supreme Court . . . [Wilmington, Printed by James Adams, 1782]. § 4 p.; fol.

Passed at Dover, February 5, 1782.

Bristol (Evans 44190); Hawkins B:17.
Copies: DLC; MdBP; NNB; PPL.

157. DELAWARE. LAWS.

Anno millesimo septingentesimo octogesimo secundo. An act for the protection of the trade of this State on the river and bay of Delaware. [Wilmington, Printed by James Adams, 1782]. § 4 p.; fol.

Passed February 5, 1782.

Bristol (Evans 44192); Hawkins B:16.
Copies: DLC; MdBP; NNB; PPL.

158. DELAWARE. LT. GOVERNOR.
By the Vice-President of the Delaware State. A proclamation . . . Given at New-Castle, on the fourteenth day of November, 1782. John Cook, Vice-President. [Wilmington, Printed by James Adams, 1782]. § Broadside.

Offering a reward of fifty dollars for the apprehension of Bartholomew Baynum.

Evans 17519.
No copy known.

159. FOX, THOMAS.
The Wilmington almanack, or ephemeris, for the year of our Lord 1783 . . . Wilmington, Printed and sold by James Adams [1782]. § [36] p.; 12mo.

Evans 17535.
Copies: DLC; DeHi; DeWI; MWA.

1783

160. At a meeting of deputies, chosen in and for each hundred of Kent County, in the Delaware State, at Dover, on Monday the first day of September, 1783 . . . Resolved, that . . . the people ought strictly to regard the political character of their representatives . . . [Wilmington, Printed by James Adams? 1783]. § Broadside; 21 by 17 cm.

Bristol (Evans 44392); Hawkins C:12.
Copies: DLC.

161. BAPTISTS.
Summary of church discipline, shewing the qualifications and duties of the officers and members of a Gospel-Church. By the

Baptist-Association in Charlestown, South-Carolina . . . Wilmington, Printed by James Adams, 1783. § [4], 47 p.; 8vo.

Evans 17826.
Copies: DLC.

162. BARCLAY, ROBERT, 1648–1690.
The anarchy of the ranters, and other libertines; the hierarchy of the Romanists, and other pretended churches, equally refused and refuted, in a two-fold apology for the church and people of God, called in derision, Quakers . . . Wilmington, Re-printed by James Adams, 1783. § vii, [1], 111 p.; 8vo.

Part of: Three treatises.

Evans 17827.
Copies: DLC; DeGE; DeHi; DeU; DeWF; DeWI; DeWin; MWA; NN; PBL; PBm; PHC; PPL.

163. DELAWARE. GENERAL ASSEMBLY. HOUSE.
Votes and proceedings of the House of Assembly of the Delaware State, held at Dover on Monday the 21st day of October, 1782. Wilmington, Printed by James Adams, in High-Street, 1783. § 17, [1] p.; fol.

Evans 17910.
Copies: De; DeWI.

164. DELAWARE. GENERAL ASSEMBLY. HOUSE.
Votes of the House of Assembly of the Delaware State. Dover, Monday, January 6, 1783. [Wilmington, Printed by James Adams, 1783]. § 19–75, [1] p.; fol.

Evans 17911.
Copies: De; DeWI.

165. DELAWARE. GENERAL ASSEMBLY. HOUSE.
Votes of the House of Assembly of the Delaware State. Monday, May 26, 1783. [Wilmington, Printed by James Adams, 1783]. § 77–119, [1] p.; fol.

Evans 17912.
Copies: De; DeWI.

166. DELAWARE. GENERAL ASSEMBLY. HOUSE.
Votes and proceedings of the House of Assembly of the Delaware State . . . October, 1783. [Wilmington, Printed by James Adams, 1783?].

Evans 17913.
No copy known.

167. DELAWARE. GOVERNOR.
By His Excellency Nicholas Vandyke, Esq.; President, of the Delaware State, a proclamation . . . [appointing a day of thanksgiving for the success of our arms.] Given . . . the seventeenth day of November . . . 1783. Wilmington, Printed by James Adams [1783]. § Broadside.

Signed in mss: Nicholas Vandyke, President.

Evans 17909.
Copies: NN.

168. DELAWARE. LAWS.
Acts of the General Assembly of the Delaware State, at a session begun at Dover on the twentieth day of October 1782, and continued by adjournments [to June 21, 1783]: being their seventh session. Wilmington, Printed by James Adams, 1783. § 29 p.; fol.

Evans 17906; 17908.
Copies: DLC; MdBP; NNB; PPL.

169. DELAWARE. LAWS.
Laws enacted by the General Assembly of the State of Delaware, which commenced at Dover, on Monday the sixth day of January, in the year of our Lord one thousand seven [hundred] and eighty-three. [Wilmington, Printed by James Adams, 1783]. § 4 p.; fol.

Bristol, p. 341; Evans 17907.
Copies: DLC; NNB; PPL.

170. Essay on marriage; or, The lawfulness of divorce, in certain cases, considered. Addressed to the feelings of mankind. Wilmington, Re-printed by James Adams, 1783. § 28 p.; 8vo.

Copies: DeWI.

171. FINLEY, JAMES.
A brief attempt to set the prohibition in the XVIIIth and XXth chapters of the book of Leviticus in a proper light. Wherein an answer to the two following questions is more especially attended to, viz. I. Whether it be right for a man, after the death of his wife, to marry her sister? II. Supposing the marriage to be wrong, whether they, continuing to cohabit, may be admitted to church privileges . . . Wilmington, Printed by James Adams, 1783. § ii, 5–20 p.; 8vo.

Evans 17928; 19406.
Copies: DeHi (photocopy); DeWI; MWA; NHi; PPPrHi.

172. FOX, THOMAS.
The Wilmington almanack, or ephemeris, for the year of our Lord 1784 . . . Wilmington, Printed and sold by James Adams [1783]. § [36] p.; 8vo.

Evans 17933.
Copies: DeHi; DeWI; DeWin; InU; MWA; NHi; PHi (now in PPL).

173. PENN, WILLIAM, 1644–1718.
A brief account of the rise and progress of the people called Quakers, in which their fundamental principle, doctrines, worship, ministry and discipline are plainly declared. With a summary reltaion [!] of the former dispensations of God in the World, by way of introduction . . . The seventh edition . . . Wilmington, Reprinted by James Adams, 1783. § [6], 88 p.; 8vo.

Part of: Three treatises.

Evans 18083.
Copies: DLC; DeGE; DeHi; DeU; DeWF; DeWI; DeWin; MWA; NN; PBL; PBm; PHC; PPL; PSC.

174. PIKE, JOSEPH, 1657–1729.
An epistle to the national meeting of Friends, in Dublin, concerning good order and discipline in the Church . . . Wilmington, Re-printed by James Adams, 1783. § 24 p.; 8vo.

Part of: Three treatises.

Evans 18083.
Copies: DLC; DeGE; DeHi; DeU; DeWF; DeWI; DeWin; MWA; NN; PBL; PBm; PPL; PSC.

175. Three treatises, in which the fundamental principle, doctrines, worship, ministry, and discipline of the people called Quakers, are plainly declared. The first, by William Penn, in England; the second, by Robert Barclay, in Scotland; the third, by Joseph Pike, in Ireland. Wilmington, Re-printed by James Adams, 1783. § [8], 88, vii, [1], 111, 24 p.; 8vo.

Each treatise has separate title page and pagination.

Evans 18083.
Copies: DLC; DeGE; DeHi; DeU; DeWF; DeWI; DeWin; MWA; NN; PBL; PBm; PPL; PSC.

176. U.S. CONTINENTAL CONGRESS, 1783.
By the United States of America in Congress assembled. A proclamation, declaring the cessation of arms, as well by sea as by land, agreed upon between the United States of America and his Britannic Majesty; and enjoining the observance thereof . . . Done in Congress, at Philadelphia, this eleventh day of April, in the year of our Lord one thousand seven hundred and eighty-three, and of our sovereignty and independence the seventh. Elias Boudinot, President. Charles Thomson, Secretary. New-Castle, the fifteenth day of April, 1783. [Wilmington, Printed by James Adams, 1783]. § Broadside.

Evans 18243.
No copy known.

1784

177. DELAPLAIN, JAMES.
Notice is hereby given, that the subscriber, by a late law of this State, is appointed collector of the state-tax for the county of New-Castle . . . Wilmington, Printed by James Adams, 1784. § Broadside; 21 by 18 cm.

Dated: Newport, New-Castle County, Aug. 23, 1784, and signed: James Delaplain.

Copies: DeHi.

178. DELAWARE. GENERAL ASSEMBLY. HOUSE.
Votes and proceedings of the House of Assembly of the Delaware State . . . May, 1784. [Wilmington, Printed by James Adams, 1784].

Evans 18443.
No copy known.

179. DELAWARE. GOVERNOR.
By his Excellency Nicholas Vandyke, Esq.; President, Captain-General and Commander in Chief of the Delaware State. A proclamation. [Directing the return of all public property to the county treasurers]. Given under my hand and the great-seal of the State, at New-Castle, the twenty-second day of September, in the year of our Lord one thousand seven hundred and eighty-four, and in the ninth year of the independency of this State. Nicholas Vandyke . . . Wilmington, Printed by James Adams [1784]. § Broadside.

Evans 18442.
Copies: NN.

180. DELAWARE. LAWS.
Acts of the General Assembly of the Delaware State, at a session begun at Dover on the twentieth day of October 1783, and continued by adjournments: being their eighth session. Wilmington, Printed by James Adams, 1784. § 17 p.; fol.

Evans 18441.
Copies: DLC; MdBP; NNB; PPL.

181. DELAWARE. LAWS.
Delaware State, November 15, 1784. Public notice. Whereas by a resolution of the honourable the Continental Congress . . . have called upon this State to make up their quota of a deficiency of moneys. In conformity thereto, this State have passed a law . . .

THE
DISCOVERY, SETTLEMENT
And present State of
KENTUCKE:
AND
An ESSAY towards the TOPOGRAPHY, and NATURAL HISTORY of that important Country:

To which is added,

An APPENDIX,
CONTAINING,

I. The ADVENTURES of Col. *Daniel Boon,* one of the first Settlers, comprehending every important Occurrence in the political History of that Province.

II The MINUTES of the *Piankashaw* council, held at *Post St. Vincents,* April 15, 1784.

III. An ACCOUNT of the *Indian* Nations inhabiting within the Limits of the Thirteen United States, their Manners and Customs, and Reflections on their Origin.

IV. The STAGES and DISTANCES between *Philadelphia* and the Falls of the *Ohio*; from *Pittsburg* to *Pensacola* and several other Places. —The Whole illustrated by a new and accurate MAP of *Kentucke* and the Country adjoining, drawn from actual Surveys.

By JOHN FILSON.

Wilmington, Printed by JAMES ADAMS, 1784.

facing

auhorizing [!] three collectors for the State . . . Wilmington, Printed by James Adams [1784]. § Broadside.

Hawkins C:13; Heartman 662.
No copy known.

182.   FILSON, JOHN, 1747–1788.
    The discovery, settlement and present state of Kentucke: and An essay towards the topography, and natural history of that important country: To which is added, an appendix, containing, I. The adventures of Col. Daniel Boon . . . II. The minutes of the Piankashaw council . . . April 15, 1784. III. An account of the Indian nations . . . IV. The stages and distances between Philadelphia and the Falls of Ohio . . . The whole illustrated by a new and accurate map . . . Wilmington, Printed by James Adams, 1784. § 118p.; map; 8vo.

Map was not issued with the work at Wilmington, but printed separately at Philadelphia.

Evans 18467.
Copies: DLC; DeU; DeWI; MWA; PPAmP; PPL; PPRF; PU.

183.   FOX, THOMAS.
    The Wilmington almanack, or ephemeris, for the year of our Lord 1785 . . . Wilmington, Printed and sold by James Adams [1784]. § [36] p.; 8vo.

Evans 18478.
Copies: DeHi; DeWin; PCDHi.

184.   WILMINGTON, DEL. FRIENDSHIP FIRE COMPANY
    Articles for the Friendship Fire Company in Wilmington. [Wilmington, Printed by James Adams, 1784]. § Broadside 43 by 38 cm.

Dated: Sept. 23, 1784.

Copies: DeHi.

185. [ARMOR, SAMUEL] 1766–1831.
Oratio salutatoria suffr. ampliss. facult. philos. praeside viro celeber. Domino Gulielmo Smith, habita in alma Acad. Wash. die decimo quarto Maii, anno Dom. M,DCC,LXXXIII. Wilmingtoni, Impressa a Jacobo Adams, 1785. § vii, 9–16 p.; front.; 8vo.

Evans 18916; Sabin 84630 (attributed to William Smith).
Copies: DLC; PHi (now in PPL); PU.

186. BOEHME, ANTON WILHELM, 1673–1722.
Spiritual improvement of temporal affliction: a sermon. To which is annexed, a prayer, for a right improvement of afflictions. By the Revd. Anthony W. Boehm [!] . . . Wilmington, Printed and sold by James Adams, 1785. § 36 p.; 8vo.

Evans 18935.
Copies: PHi.

187. The Christian oeconomy. Translated from the original Greek manuscript found on the island of Patmos. Wilmington, Printed by James Adams, 1785. § xii, 13–36 p.; 12mo.

Copies: DeHi; PU.

188. DELAWARE. GENERAL ASSEMBLY. HOUSE.
Votes and proceedings of the House of Assembly of the Delaware State, held at Dover, on Wednesday, the twentieth day of October, in the year of our Lord, one thousand seven hundred and eighty-four. Wilmington, Printed by Jacob A. Killen and Co., in Market-Street, opposite the Post-Office [1785]. § 15, [1] p.; fol.

Evans 18988.
Copies: De; PHi (now in PPL).

189. DELAWARE. GENERAL ASSEMBLY. HOUSE.
Votes of the House of Assembly of the Delaware State. Dover, Monday, January 3, 1785. [Wilmington, Printed by Jacob A. Killen and Co., 1785]. § 17–61 p.; fol.

Evans 18989.
Copies: De; PHi (now in PPL).

190. DELAWARE. GENERAL ASSEMBLY. HOUSE.

Votes and proceedings of the House of Assembly of the Delaware State, held at Dover, on Monday the sixteenth day of May, in the year of our Lord one thousand seven hundred and eighty-five. Wilmington, Printed by Jacob A. Killen and Co., 1785. § 25 p.; fol.

Evans 18990.
Copies: De; DeHi; DeWI; PHi (now in PPL).

191. DELAWARE. GENERAL ASSEMBLY. HOUSE.

Votes and proceedings of the House of Assembly of the Delaware State . . . September, 1785. [Wilmington, Printed by Jacob A. Killen and Co., 1785].

Evans 18991.
No copy known; probably none published, cf. Shipton, Evans' microcard ed.

192. DELAWARE. GOVERNOR.

By his Excellency Nicholas Vandyke, Esq.; President, Captain-General and Commander in Chief of the Delaware State. A proclamation. [Offering a reward of one hundred pounds for the apprehension of certain named burglars]. Given . . . the second day of August, in the year of our Lord one thousand seven hundred and eighty-five. Wilmington, Printed by Jacob A. Killen & Co. on the west side of Market-Street, opposite the Post-Office [1785]. § Broadside; 33 by 21 cm.

Evans 18987.
Copies: DLC.

193. DELAWARE. GOVERNOR.

Delaware State, ss. His Excellency, the President, having received the following act of Congress of the 17th of March last, orders that the same be made public throughout this State. James Booth, Secretary. New-Castle, May 5, 1785. By the United States, in Congress assembled, March 17, 1785 . . . Wilmington, Printed by Jacob A. Killen & Co. in Market Street, opposite the Post-Office [1785]. § Broadside; 42 by 26 cm.

A resolution requiring all persons to deliver abstracts of claims against the United States.

Bristol (Evans 44675); Hawkins C:14.
Copies: DLC; MWA.

194. DELAWARE. LAWS.
Acts of the General Assembly of the Delaware State, at a session begun at Dover on the twentieth day of October 1784, and continued by adjournments: being their ninth session. Wilmington, Printed by James Adams, 1785. § 27 p.; fol.

Evans 18984.
Copies: DLC; NNB; PPL.

195. DELAWARE. LAWS.
Acts of the General Assembly of the Delaware State, at an adjourned session . . . May, 1785. Wilmington, Printed by Jacob A. Killen and Co., 1785. § 20 p.; fol.

Evans 18985; probably same as no. 197.
No copy known.

196. DELAWARE. LAWS.
Acts of the General Assembly of the Delaware State . . . September, 1785. [Wilmington, Printed by Jacob A. Killen and Co., 1785].

Evans 18986.
No copy known; probably none published, cf. Shipton, Evans' microcard ed.

197. DELAWARE. LAWS.
Laws of the General Assembly of the Delaware State. At a General Assembly of the Delaware State, commenced at Dover the 20th day of October, 1784, and continued by adjournment till the fourth day of June, 1785: being their tenth session. Wilmington, Printed by Jacob A. Killen & Co., 1785. § 20 p.; fol.

Evans 18985; Hawkins B:18.
Copies: DLC; NNB; PPAmP.

198.	The Delaware gazette. June 14 [–December, 1785]. Wilmington, Printed by Jacob A. Killen, on the west side of Market-Street, opposite the Post-Office, 1785. § fol.; weekly.

Title was altered to *The Delaware gazette; or The Faithful centinel* between June 28, 1785 and Jan. 18, 1786.

Brigham, v. 1, p. 80; Evans 18992.
Copies: DeHi (microfilm); NHi.

199.	Fox, Thomas.
	The Wilmington almanack, or ephemeris, for the year of our Lord 1786 . . . Wilmington, Printed and sold by James Adams [1785]. § [36] p.; 12mo.

Evans 19008.
Copies: DLC; DeHi; DeWI; MWA; NHi; PHi (now in PPL).

200.	Hemphill, William, 1743–1823.
	Advertisement. Whereas the partnership of Wade and Hemphill has been expired upwards of eight years, and many persons are yet indebted to said partnership . . . this . . . is to acquaint all persons indebted to said partnership . . . that the whole list of debts will be delivered into the hands of a lawyer . . . Wilmington, Printed by James Adams, 1785. § Broadside; 26 by 18 cm.

Dated above the text: Wilmington, April 20, 1785; signed: William Hemphill.

Copies: DeHi.

201.	Presbyterian Church in the U.S.A. Presbytery of New Castle.
	An address from the Presbytery of New-Castle to the congregations under their care: setting forth the declining state of religion in their bounds; and exciting them to the duties necessary for a revival of decayed piety amongst them. Published by order of the Presbytery, convened at Upper Octorora, August 11, 1784, William Smith, moderator . . . Wilmington, Printed by James Adams, 1785. § 62 p.; 8vo.

Evans 19199.
Copies: DLC; DeHi (photocopy); DeWI (photocopy); MWA; NHi; PPAmP.

202. A synopsis of geography, with the use of the terrestrial globe, intended for the benefit of youth, especially that of the students in the public grammar school in Wilmington. Wilmington, Printed by James Adams, 1785. § 58 p.; 8vo.

Bristol (Evans 44796); Hawkins B:19.
Copies: DeWI; MWA.

1786

203. ADAMS, JAMES.
To the public. As the advantages arising from well executed newspapers appear to be universally acknowledged . . . the subscribers . . . content themselves with offering the following proposals for publishing in Wilmington, Delaware State, The Delaware courant, and Weekly advertiser. Wilmington [Printed by James Adams, junior, and Samuel Adams, 1786]. § Broadside; 45 by 25 cm.

Signed: James (jun.) and Samuel Adams, Wilmington, May 17, 1786.

Evans 19449.
Copies: PHi.

204. DELAWARE. GENERAL ASSEMBLY. HOUSE.
Votes and proceedings of the House of Assembly of the Delaware State, commenced at Dover, on Thursday, the twentieth day of October, in the year of our Lord one thousand seven hundred and eighty-five [to February 3, 1786]. Wilmington, Printed by Jacob A. Killen & Co., 1786. § 50 p.; fol.

Evans 19602.
Copies: DLC; De; MHi; PHi (now in PPL).

205. DELAWARE. GENERAL ASSEMBLY. HOUSE.
Votes and proceedings of the House of Assembly of the Delaware State, at a session commenced at Dover, on Tuesday the twenty-third day of May, in the year of our Lord one thousand seven hundred and eighty-six. Wilmington, Printed by Jacob A.

Killen, in Market-Street, west side, above Second-Street, 1786. §
36 p.; fol.

Evans 19603.
Copies: De; PHi (now in PPL).

206. DELAWARE. GENERAL ASSEMBLY. HOUSE.
Votes and proceedings of the House of Assembly of the Delaware State, at a session commenced at Dover, on Friday, the
twentieth day of October, in the year of our Lord one thousand
seven hundred and eighty-six. Wilmington, Printed by Jacob A.
Killen, in Market-Street, west side, above Second-Street, 1786. §
17 p.; fol.

Evans 19604.
Copies: De; DeHi (incomplete); PHi (now in PPL).

207. DELAWARE. LAWS.
Laws of the General Assembly, of the Delaware State, at a
General Assembly of the Delaware State, commenced at Dover, on
the twentieth day of October, 1785, and continued by adjournment
'till the third day of February, 1786, inclusive: being their eleventh
session. Wilmington, Printed by Jacob A. Killen & Co., 1786. §
19 p.; fol.

Evans 19600.
Copies: DLC; DeHi; NNB; PPAmP.

208. DELAWARE. LAWS.
Laws of the General Assembly, of the Delaware State, at a
General Assembly of the Delaware State, commenced at Dover, on
the twenty-third day of May, in the year of our Lord, one thousand
seven hundred and eighty-six: being their twelfth session. Wilmington, Printed by Jacob A. Killen & Co. in Market-Street, west
side, 1786. § 12 p.; fol.

Evans 19601.
Copies: DLC; DeHi; NNB; PPAmP.

209. The Delaware courant, and Wilmington advertiser. Vol. 1,
no. 1, September [–December, 1786]. Wilmington, Printed
by Samuel and John Adams, in High-Street, 1786. § fol.; weekly.

Earliest issue located: Vol. 1, no. 35, May 5, 1787.

Brigham, v. 1, p. 80; Evans 19605.
Copies: MWA.

210.   The Delaware gazette. January [–December, 1786]. Wilmington, Printed by Jacob A. Killen, on the west side of Market-Street, between Third and High Streets, 1786. § fol.; weekly.

Title was altered to *The State gazette, or The Faithful centinel* in July or August, 1786. It was changed back to *The Delaware gazette* between November, 1786, and March, 1787.

Brigham, v. 1, p. 80–81; Evans 19606.
Copies: DeHi; MWA.

211.   FOX, THOMAS.
The Wilmington almanack, or ephemeris, for the year of our Lord, 1787 . . . Wilmington, Printed and sold by James Adams [1786]. § [36] p.; 12mo.

Evans 19653.
Copies: DLC; DeHi; DeWI; DeWin; MWA; P; PHi (now in PPL).

212.   HAYWARD, SAMUEL.
An important case of conscience answered, at the casuistical lecture, in Little St. Helen's, Bishopgate-Street, London. By the Rev. S. Hayward . . . London, Printed; Wilmington, Re-printed and sold by James Adams, 1786. § 17 p.; 8vo.

Evans 19707.
Copies: DeWI; PHi (now in PPL).

213.   HENRY, MATTHEW, 1662–1714.
Prayers in Scripture expressions; for the use of families. To which are annexed, a number of prayers in other language [!], upon most occasions . . . Wilmington, Printed by James Adams, 1786. § x, 11–204 p.; 12mo.

Bristol (Evans 44901); Hawkins B:20.
Copies: DLC; De(M); DeHi; DeWI.

214. M'WILLIAM, REBECCA.
Notice. To be sold, by publick vendue, on Thursday the
seventeeth day of August instant, at the late dwelling-house of
Richard M'William, Esq., deceased, in the town of New-Castle . . .
Rebecca M'William, executrix . . . New-Castle, August 3, 1786.
N.B. The said executors will, at private sale, dispose of three sev-
eral plantations . . . Wilmington, Printed by Jacob A. Killen &
Co., on the west side of Market-Street, between Third and High-
Streets [1786]. § Broadside.

Evans 19873.
Copies: NN.

215. WILMINGTON ACADEMY.
Draught of a plan of education for the Wilmington Academy, which was adopted by the trustees of the said Academy at
their meeting on the 2d and 22d day of May, 1786. [Wilmington,
Printed by James Adams, 1786]. § 8 p.; 8vo.

Evans 20149.
Copies: DeWI; PHi (now in PPL); RPJCB.

1787
_____

216. BIBLE. N.T.
The New Testament of our Lord and Saviour Jesus Christ:
Newly translated out of the original Greek; and with the former
translations diligently compared and revised. Wilmington, Printed
and sold by James Adams, in High-Street, 1787. § [335] p.; 12mo.

Bristol (Evans 45039); Hawkins B:21.
Copies: DeWI; DeWin.

217. DELAWARE. GENERAL ASSEMBLY. HOUSE.
Votes and proceedings of the House of Assembly of the Delaware State, at a session commenced at Dover, on Monday, the
eighth day of January, in the year of our Lord one thousand seven
hundred and eighty-seven. Wilmington, Printed by Frederick
Craig and Co., in Market-Street, 1787. § 61 p.; fol.

Evans 20323.
Copies: De; PHi (now in PPL).

218. DELAWARE. GENERAL ASSEMBLY. HOUSE.
Votes and proceedings of the House of Assembly of the Delaware State, at a session commenced at Dover, on Monday, the twenty-eighth day of May, one thousand seven hundred and eighty-seven. Wilmington, Printed by Frederick Craig and Co. in Market-Street, 1787. § 12 p.; fol.

Evans 20324.
Copies: De; PHi (now in PPL).

219. DELAWARE. GENERAL ASSEMBLY. HOUSE.
Votes and proceedings of the House of Assembly of the Delaware State, at a session commenced at Dover, on Monday, the twenty-seventh day of August, in the year of our Lord, one thousand seven hundred and eighty-seven. Wilmington, Printed by Frederick Craig & Co., in Market-Street, 1787. § [2], 29 p.; fol.

Evans 20325.
Copies: De; PHi (now in PPL).

220. DELAWARE. GENERAL ASSEMBLY. SENATE.
Votes and proceedings of the Legislative Council of the Delaware State, at a session commenced at Dover, on Monday, the twentieth day of October, in the year of our Lord one thousand seven hundred and eighty-three. Wilmington, Printed by James Adams, in High-Street, 1787. § 219 p.; fol.

Contains the minutes of the sessions beginning on Oct. 20, 1783; Jan. 5, March 29, May 24, Oct. 20, 1784; Jan. 3, May 16, Oct. 20, 1785; Jan. 3, May 29, Oct. 20, 1786; Jan. 9, May 28, 1787.

Copies: De.

221. DELAWARE. GENERAL ASSEMBLY. SENATE.
Votes and proceedings of the Legislative Council of the Delaware State, October 20th, 1787. Wilmington, Printed by Frederick Craig and Co. in Market-Street, 1787. § 24 p.; fol.
Copies: De.

222. DELAWARE. LAWS.

Laws of the General Assembly of the Delaware State, at a session commenced at Dover on the twentieth day of October, 1786, and continued by adjournments: being their twelfth session. Wilmington, Printed by James Adams, 1787. § 33 p.; fol.

Evans 20320.

Copies: DLC; DeHi; NNB; PPAmP.

223. DELAWARE. LAWS.

Laws of the General Assembly of the Delaware State, at a session commenced at Dover, on the twentieth day of October 1786, and continued by adjournments: being their twelfth session [28 May–8 June, 1787]. Wilmington, Printed by James Adams, 1787. § 7 p.; fol.

Evans 20321.

Copies: DLC; NNB; PPAmP.

224. DELAWARE. LAWS.

Laws of the General Assembly of the Delaware State, at a session commenced at Dover on the twentieth day of October, 1787, and continued by adjournments: being their thirteenth session. Wilmington, Printed by James Adams, 1787. § 9 p.; fol.

Evans 20322.

Copies: DLC; NNB; PPAmP.

225. The Delaware almanack, or Eastern Shore calendar, for the year 1788 . . . Wilmington, Printed by Frederick Craig and Co. [1787]. § [36] p.; 12mo.

Evans 20326.

Copies: DLC; DeHi; InU; MWA; NjP.

226. The Delaware courant, and Wilmington advertiser. Vol. 1, no. 18, Saturday, January 6 [–vol. 2, no. 53, Saturday, September 8, 1787?]. Wilmington, Printed by Samuel and John Adams, in High-Street, 1787. § fol.; weekly.

Last issue located: September 8, 1787, cf. Brigham.

Brigham, v. 1, p. 80; Evans 20327.

Copies: DeHi (microfilm); MWA.

227.   The Delaware gazette; or The Faithful centinel. No. 82,
Wednesday, January 3 [–no. 133, Wednesday, December
26, 1787]. Wilmington, Printed and published by Frederick Craig
and Company in Market-Street, three doors below the Indian King,
1787. § fol.; weekly.
Evans 20328.
Copies: DLC; DeHi (microfilm); MWA.

228.   Fox, Thomas.
The Wilmington almanack, or ephemeris, for the year of
our Lord 1788 . . . Wilmington, Printed and sold by James Adams
[1787]. § [36] p.; 12mo.
Evans 20366.
Copies: DLC; P.

229.   Fox, Thomas.
The Wilmington pocket almanack, for the year 1788 . . .
Wilmington, Printed and sold by James Adams [1787]. § 28 p.;
12mo.
Bristol (Evans 45068); Drake 1375; Hawkins B:22.
Copies: DLC.

230.   Killen, William, 1722–1805.
Proposals for compiling and printing a new edition of the
Delaware laws, in two folio volumes . . . Wilmington, Printed by
Jacob A. Killen, on the west side of Market-Street, between Third
and High-Streets [1787]. § Broadside; 45 by 30 cm.

Dated: Dover, February 14, 1787.

Evans 20443.
Copies: PHi.

231.   Pattillo, Henry, 1726–1801.
The plain planter's family assistant; containing an address
to husbands and wives, children and servants. With some helps for
instruction by catechisms; and examples of devotion for families:
with a brief paraphrase on the Lord's prayer. By Henry Pattillo . . .
Wilmington, Printed by James Adams, 1787. § vi, 7–63 p.; 12mo.
Copies: PHi (now in PPL); PPPrHi.

232.   This indenture witnesseth, that——hath put h——appren-
tice to——. Wilmington, Printed by Jacob A. Killen & Co.
in Market-Street, opposite the Post-Office [1787]. § Broadside;
32 by 20 cm.

Pen dated: Aug. 18, 1787.

Hawkins C:15.
Copies: DeHi.

233.   U.S. CONSTITUTION.
We, the people of the United States, in order to form a more
perfect union . . . do ordain and establish this Constitution for the
United States of America . . . Wilmington, Frederick Craig & Co.
[1787]. § [3] p.; fol.

Bristol (Evans 45179).
Copies: PPL.

1788

234.   An address to the legislators of the states of North America.
By a peace-maker . . . Wilmington, Printed by Frederick
Craig & Co., 1788. § [3], 4–27 p.; 8vo.

Copies: RPJCB.

235.   COLLEY, THOMAS, 1742–1812.
A sermon, publicly delivered, on 3d day morning, the 8th
day of the 5th month, 1787 at a public meeting of the people called
Quakers, held in Market-Street, Philadelphia. Wilmington, Printed by Frederick Craig & Co., 1788. § 16 p.; 8vo.

Copies: PHC; PHi (now in PPL).

236.   The Columbian almanac for town and country for 1789.
Wilmington [1788].

Drake 1376.
No copy known.

237. DELAWARE. GENERAL ASSEMBLY. HOUSE.
Votes and proceedings of the House of Assembly of the Delaware State, at a session commenced at Dover on Monday the seventh day of January, in the year of our Lord one thousand seven hundred and eighty-eight. Wilmington, Printed by James Adams and Sons, in High-Street, 1788. § 43 p.; fol.

Evans 21050.
Copies: De; PHi (now in PPL).

238. DELAWARE. GENERAL ASSEMBLY. HOUSE.
Votes and proceedings of the House of Assembly of the Delaware State, at a session commenced at Dover, on Tuesday the twenty-seventh day of May, in the year of our Lord one thousand seven hundred and eighty-eight. Wilmington, Printed by Frederick Craig and Co., in Market-Street, 1788. § 37 p.; fol.

Evans 21051.
Copies: De; PHi (now in PPL).

239. DELAWARE. GENERAL ASSEMBLY. HOUSE.
Votes and proceedings of the House of Assembly of the Delaware State, at a session commenced at Dover on Monday the twentieth day of October, in the year of our Lord one thousand seven hundred and eighty-eight. Wilmington, Printed by James Adams and Sons, in High-Street, 1788. § 16 p.; fol.

Evans 21052.
Copies: De; PHi (now in PPL).

240. DELAWARE. LAWS.
Laws of the General Assembly of the Delaware State, at a session commenced at Dover on the twentieth day of October, 1787, and continued by adjournments. Wilmington, Printed by Frederick Craig and Co., in Market-Street, 1788. § 7 p.; fol.

Evans 21047.
Copies: DLC; NNB; PPAmP.

241. DELAWARE. LAWS.
Laws of the Delaware State, passed at a session of the General Assembly commenced at Dover, on the twenty-seventh day of

May, 1788. Wilmington, Printed by James Adams and Sons, 1788. § 22 p.; fol.

Evans 21048.
Copies: DLC; NNB; PPAmP.

242. DELAWARE. LAWS.
Laws of the Delaware State, passed at a session of the General Assembly, commenced at Dover, on the 20th day of October, 1788. Wilmington, Printed by Frederick Craig & Co., in Market-Street [1788]. § 7 p.; fol.

Evans 21049.
Copies: DLC; NNB; PPAmP.

243. The Delaware gazette; or The Faithful centinel. No. 134, Wednesday, January 2 [–no. 184, Saturday, December 27, 1788]. Wilmington, Printed and published by Frederick Craig and Company, at their office in Market Street, 1788. § fol.; weekly.

Evans 21053.
Copies: DeHi; MWA.

244. The Federal almanac for the year 1789 . . . adapted to the latitude and longitude of Wilmington, in the state of Delaware . . . Wilmington, Printed by Frederick Craig and Co. [1788]. § [36] p.; 12mo.

Bristol (Evans 45256); Drake 1378; Hawkins B:24.
Copies: DeWin; PHi (now in PPL).

245. FOX, THOMAS.
The Wilmington almanack, or ephemeris, for the year of our Lord 1789 . . . Wilmington, Printed and sold by James Adams [1788]. § [36] p.; 12mo.

Evans 21094.
Copies: DLC; DeHi; DeWI; MWA; MiU-C; PHi (now in PPL).

246. FOX, THOMAS.
The Wilmington pocket almanack for the year 1789 . . . Wilmington, Printed and sold by James Adams [1788]. § [28] p.; 24mo.

Interleaved with blank leaves.

Copies: MWA.

247. The New England primer, with the shorter catechism. Wilmington, Printed and sold by James Adams, 1788. § 79 p.; illus.; 16mo.

Copies: DeWin.

248. PATTILLO, HENRY, 1726–1801.
Sermons, &c. I. On the divisions among Christians. II. On the necessity of regeneration to future happiness. III. The Scripture doctrine of election. IV. Extract of a letter from Mr. Whitefield to Mr. Wesley. V. An address to the deists . . . Wilmington, Printed by James Adams, for the author, 1788. § xii, 13–295 p.; 12mo.

Evans 21361.
Copies: DeHi; DeU; DeWI; MWA; NHi; NN; PHi; PPPrHi.

249. The plain planter and farmer's family assistant: containing an address to husbands and wives, children and servants; with three catechisms, for children, youths, and Negroes. Wilmington, Printed and sold by James Adams & Sons, 1788.

Evans 21397; probably same as no. 231.
No copy known.

250. Second notice for public information . . . Sales of the real estate of the late Mr. John Vangezell of New-Castle . . . George Read, executor. New Castle, March 20, 1788. Wilmington, Printed by Frederick Craig and Co. [1788]. § Broadside; 18 by 22 cm.

Copies: DeWI.

251. The storekeeper's and mechanic's sheet almanac for the year of our Lord 1789. Wilmington, Printed by James Adams [1788]. § Broadside?

"Item 257 from Catalogue 576 (1926) of C. W. Unger (Pottsville)"—Note on card in N.Y. Pub. Libr. imprint file.

Bristol, p. 400; Hawkins C:16.
No copy known.

252.   VAN CUELEN, JACOBUS.
The Delaware almanack, or Eastern Shore calendar for the
year 1789 . . . Wilmington, Printed by Frederick Craig and Co.
[1788]. § [36] p.; 8vo.

Drake 1373; Evans 21536.
Copies: DLC; InU; MWA; NjP; P.

253.   WILMINGTON, DEL. LIBRARY COMPANY.
An act to incorporate the members of the Library Company
of Wilmington. [Wilmington, Printed by James Adams, 1788].
§ 32 p; 8vo.

At head of title: In the twelfth year of the independence of the Delaware State.

Catalogue of books: p. 13–32.

Evans 21046.
Copies: DeWI; MWA.

1789

254.   [BURKE, ANN].
Ela: or The delusions of the heart. A tale founded on facts.
Wilmington, Printed and sold by Brynberg, and Andrews, at the
Post-Office, Market-Street, 1789. § 140, ii p.; 12mo.

Bristol (Evans 45445).
Copies: CSmH.

255.   CHESTERFIELD, PHILIP DORMER STANHOPE, 4TH
        EARL OF, 1694–1773.
Lord Chesterfield's advice to his son, on men and manners; or, A
new system of education . . . To which are annexed, The polite
philosopher . . . also, Lord Burghley's Ten precepts to his second
son, Robert Cecil, afterwards the Earl of Salisbury. Wilmington,
Printed by James Adams, 1789. § 106 p.; 12mo.

Bristol (Evans 45450).
Copies: DeWI; PPL.

256.   The Columbian almanac; or, The North-American calendar,
        for the year of our Lord, 1790 . . . Wilmington, Printed and
sold by Peter Brynberg and Samuel Andrews, at the Post-Office in
Market-Street [1789]. § [48] p.; 12mo.

Evans 21743; Hawkins B:25.
Copies: DeHi; DeWI.

257.   DELAWARE. GENERAL ASSEMBLY. HOUSE.
        Votes and proceedings of the House of Assembly of the Del-
aware State, at a session commenced at Dover, on Monday the
twelfth day of January, in the year of our Lord one thousand seven
hundred and eighty-nine. Wilmington, Printed by Frederick Craig
and Co., 1789. § 57 p.; fol.

Evans 21791.
Copies: De; PHi (now in PPL).

258.   DELAWARE. GENERAL ASSEMBLY. HOUSE.
        Votes and proceedings of the House of Assembly of the Del-
aware State, at a session commenced at Dover on Tuesday the
twenty-sixth day of May, in the year of our Lord one thousand
seven hundred and eighty-nine. Wilmington, Printed by James
Adams & Sons, in High-Street, 1789. § 17 p.; fol.

Evans 21792.
Copies: De; PHi (now in PPL).

259.   DELAWARE. GENERAL ASSEMBLY. HOUSE.
        Votes and proceedings of the House of Assembly of the Del-
aware State, at a session commenced at Dover, on Tuesday the
twentieth day of October, in the year of our Lord one thousand
seven hundred and eighty-nine. Wilmington, Printed by Frederick
Craig and Co., 1789. § 17 p.; fol.

Evans 22455 (incorrectly dated 1790).
Copies: De; PHi (now in PPL).

260. DELAWARE. LAWS.

Laws of the Delaware State, passed at a session of the General Assembly, commenced at Dover, on the twelfth day of January, 1789. Wilmington, Printed by James Adams and Sons, 1789. § 32 p.; fol.

Evans 21789.
Copies: DLC; NNB; PPAmP.

261. DELAWARE. LAWS.

Laws of the Delaware State, passed at a session of the General Assembly, commenced at Dover, on the twenty-sixth day of May, 1789. Wilmington, Printed by Frederick Craig and Co., in Market-Street [1789]. § 14 p.; fol.

Evans 21790.
Copies: DLC; NNB; PPAmP.

262. The Delaware almanac or Eastern Shore calendar for 1790 . . . by Benjamin Copernicus, philom. [pseud.?] . . . Wilmington, Printed by Frederick Craig and Co. [1789]. § [26] p.; 12mo.

Drake 1380.
Copies: MWA.

263. The Delaware gazette. No. 185, Saturday, January 3 [–no. 248, Saturday, December 26, 1789]. Wilmington, Printed and published by Frederick Craig and Company, at their office in Market-Street, 1789. § fol.; weekly.

Between May and September the title was changed to *Delaware gazette, and general advertiser*; published semi-weekly from September 2 to November 21.

Evans 21793.
Copies: DeHi; MWA.

264. [DODSLEY, ROBERT] 1703–1764.

Oeconomy of human life, complete. In two parts; translated from an Indian manuscript, written by an ancient Bramin. To which is prefixed, an account of the manner in which the said manuscript was discovered; in a letter from an English gentleman residing in China, to the Earl of . . . Wilmington, Printed by James Adams, 1789. § xv, 94, [2] p.; 12mo.

Copies: DeWI.

265. FOX, THOMAS.
The Delaware pocket almanac for the year 1790. Wilmington, Printed and sold by James Adams [1789]. § [36] p.; 12mo.

Drake 1381.
Copies: DeWin.

266. FOX, THOMAS.
The Wilmington almanack, or ephemeris, for the year of our Lord, 1790 . . . Wilmington, Printed and sold wholesale and retail, by James Adams [1789]. § 48 p.; 12mo.

Evans 21833.
Copies: DeHi; DeWin; PHi (now in PPL).

267. The glory of the Heavenly City, and the blessedness of departed saints, gracefully manifested in a vision to a young lady of Bristol, on the 10th of October, 1781. As related by herself. Wilmington, Re-printed by Brynberg and Andrews, at office, Market Street, 1789. § 28 p.; 16mo.

Bristol (Evans 45483); Hawkins B:27.
Copies: DeHi.

268. The North American pocket almanac for . . . 1790. Wilmington, Printed by Brynberg and Andrews [1789]. § [32] p.; 16mo.

Bristol (Evans 45543); Drake 1382.
Copies: MWA.

269. U.S. CONSTITUTION.
Plan of the federal government agreed to by a Convention of the United States of America on the 7th of September 1787, and since ratified by eleven of them; to which are added, the duties imposed on foreign goods by the Congress of the United States at

their present session. Wilmington, Printed by Frederick Craig and Co., 1789.

Advertised in *Delaware gazette*, Oct. 31, 1789, as "just published and to be sold by the printer hereof."

Bristol (Evans 45687); Hawkins B:28.
No copy known.

270. VAN CUELEN, JACOBUS.
    The Delaware almanac, or Eastern Shore calendar, for the year of our Lord 1790 . . . [by Jacobus Van Cuelen]. Wilmington, Printed by Frederick Craig and Co. [1789]. § [26] p.

Evans 22215.
No copy known.

271. VAN CUELEN, JACOBUS.
    The Federal almanac for the year 1790 . . . By Jacobus Van Ceulen [!], philom. Wilmington, Printed by Frederick Craig and Co. [1789]. § [36] p.; 8vo.

Bristol (Evans 45729); Hawkins B:26.
Copies: MWA.

272. WILMINGTON, DEL. LIBRARY COMPANY.
    A catalogue of the books belonging to the Library Company of Wilmington. Wilmington, Printed by Brynberg and Andrews, at the Post-Office, Market-Street, 1789. § 19 p.; 12mo.

Bristol (Evans 45750); Hawkins B:29.
Copies: CSmH; DeWI.

1790

273. The Columbian almanac; or, The North-American calendar for the year of our Lord, 1791 . . . Wilmington, Printed and sold by Andrews, Craig and Brynberg, at the Post-Office in Market Street [1790]. § [48] p.; 12mo.

Evans 22411.
Copies: DeHI; DeWI; DeWin; MWA; NHi.

274. The Columbian pocket almanac for the year 1791 . . . Wilmington, Printed and sold by Andrews, Craig and Brynberg, at the Post-Office, Market Street [1790]. § [24] p.; 12mo.

Evans 22412.
Copies: DLC.

275. DELAWARE. GENERAL ASSEMBLY. HOUSE.
Votes and proceedings of the House of Assembly of the Delaware State, at a session commenced at Dover, on Monday the fourth day of January, in the year of our Lord one thousand seven hundred and ninety. Wilmington, Printed by James Adams, in High-Street, 1790. § 47 p.; fol.

Evans 22456 ("Printed by Frederick Craig and Co.").
Copies: De; PHi (now in PPL).

276. DELAWARE. GENERAL ASSEMBLY. HOUSE.
Votes and proceedings of the House of Assembly of the Delaware State, at a session commenced at Dover, on Wednesday the twentieth day of October, in the year of our Lord one thousand seven hundred and ninety. Wilmington, Printed by Frederick Craig & Co. in Market-Street, 1790. § 17 p.; fol.

Evans 22457 ("Printed by James Adams").
Copies: De; DeHi; PHi (now in PPL).

277. DELAWARE. LAWS.
Laws of the Delaware State, passed at a session of the General Assembly, commenced at Dover, on the 20th day of October, 1789. Wilmington, Printed by Frederick Craig and Co., 1790. § 5 p.; fol.

Evans 22452.
Copies: DLC; NNB.

278. DELAWARE. LAWS.
Laws of the Delaware State, passed at a session of the General Assembly, commenced at Dover, on the fourth day of January, 1790. Wilmington, Printed by Frederick Craig and Co., 1790. § 19 p.; fol.

Evans 22453.
Copies: DLC; NNB.

279.   DELAWARE. LAWS.
     Laws of the Delaware State, passed at a session of the General Assembly, commenced at Dover, on the twentieth day of October, 1790. Wilmington, Printed by James Adams, 1790. § 13 p.; fol.

Evans 22454.
Copies: DLC; NNB; PPAmP.

280.   The Delaware gazette, and general advertiser. No. 249, Saturday, January 2 [–no. 300, Saturday, December 25, 1790]. Wilmington, Printed and published by Frederick Craig and Co., 1790. § fol.; weekly.

Evans 22458.
Copies: De (microfilm); DeHi (part on microfilm).

281.   EDWARDS, JONATHAN, 1703–1758.
     A careful and strict inquiry into the modern prevailing notions of that freedom of will, which is supposed to be essential to moral agency, virtue and vice, reward and punishment, praise and blame . . . The fourth edition. Wilmington, Printed and sold by James Adams, in High-Street, 1790. § xi, 299, 13 p.; 8vo.

Remarks on the Essays on the principles of morality and natural religion, in a letter to a minister of the Church of Scotland, by the Reverend Mr. Jonathan Edwards . . . 13 p. at end.

Evans 22476.
Copies: DLC; DeU; DeWI; DeWin; MWA; NjPT; PPAmP; PPPrHi; PU; RPJCB.

282.   FOX, THOMAS.
     The Wilmington almanack, or ephemeris, for the year of our Lord, 1791. Wilmington, Printed and sold by James Adams [1790].

Evans 22507.
No copy known.

283. NEW CASTLE CO., DEL.

New Castle County, in the State of Delaware. By virtue of an order of the Orphans Court . . . on . . . the . . . day of . . . being the real estate of . . . and to be sold for the payment of . . . debts . . . [Wilmington, 1790?]. § Broadside.

Dated in manuscript: Feb. 5th, 1790.

Copies: DeHi.

284. PROTESTANT EPISCOPAL CHURCH IN THE U.S.A. MARYLAND (DIOCESE).

Journal of the proceedings of a convention of the Protestant Episcopal Church in Maryland, held at Elkton, from Thursday, May 27th, to Monday, May 31st, one thousand seven hundred and ninety. Wilmington, Printed by Andrews, Craig, and Brynberg, in Market-Street, 1790. § 39 p.; 8vo.

Bristol (Evans 45981); Hawkins B:30.
Copies: DLC; MWA; NN.

285. U.S. LAWS.

Acts passed at a Congress of the United States of America, begun and held at the city of New-York, on Wednesday the fourth of March, in the year 1789, and of the independence of the United States, the thirteenth . . . Wilmington, Printed by Samuel Andrews, Frederick Craig, and Peter Brynberg, 1790. § 92 p.; fol.

Copies: DeWin.

286. U.S. LAWS.

Acts passed at the second session of the Congress of the United States of America, begun and held at the city of New-York, on Monday the fourth of January, in the year 1790 . . . Wilmington, Printed by Andrews and Brynberg, at the Post-Office, 1790. § 120 p.; fol.

Bristol (Evans 46070); Hawkins B:31.
Copies: DeHi.

287. VAN CUELEN, JACOBUS.

The Delaware almanac, or Eastern Shore calendar, for the year of our Lord 1791 . . . by Jacobus Van Cuelen. Wilmington,

J. Farrar

POLITICAL INQUIRIES:

TO WHICH IS ADDED,

A

P L A N

FOR THE

GENERAL ESTABLISHMENT

OF

S C H O O L S

THROUGHOUT THE UNITED STATES.

BY

ROBERT CORAM,

*Author of some late Pieces in the Delaware Gazette, under
the Signiture of* BRUTUS.

*Above all, watch carefully over the Education of your Children. It is from
public Schools, be assured, that come the wise Magistrates—the well
trained and courageous Soldiers—the good Fathers—the good
Husbands—the good Brothers—the good Friends—the
good Men.——*RAYNAL.

WILMINGTON:

PRINTED BY ANDREWS AND BRYNBERG,
IN MARKET-STREET.

M DCC XCI.

facing

Printed and sold by Andrews, Craig and Brynberg, at the Post-Office in Market-Street [1790]. § [36] p.; 12mo.

Evans 23011.
Copies: DLC; OCHP; PPL.

1791

288.   The Columbian almanac; or, The North-American calendar, for the year of our Lord 1792. Wilmington, Printed by Brynberg and Andrews [1791]. § [36] p.; 12mo.

Evans 23265.
Copies: DeWI.

289.   CORAM, ROBERT, d. 1796.
Political inquiries: to which is added, a plan for the general establishment of schools throughout the United States. By Robert Coram, author of some late pieces in the Delaware gazette, under the signiture [!] of Brutus . . . Wilmington, Printed by Andrews and Brynberg, in Market Street, 1791. § viii, [9]–107, [1] p.; 8vo.

Evans 23291.
Copies: DLC; DeGE; DeHi; DeU; DeWI; DeWin; MWA; PHi (now in PPL); PPAmP; PU; RPJCB.

290.   DELAWARE. GENERAL ASSEMBLY. HOUSE.
Votes and proceedings of the House of Assembly of the Delaware State, at a session commenced at Dover on Tuesday the fourth day of January, in the year of our Lord one thousand seven hundred and ninety-one. Wilmington, Printed by James Adams, in High-Street, 1791. § 56 p.; fol.

Evans 23322 ("Printed by Frederick Craig and Co.").
Copies: De; PHi (now in PPL).

291.   DELAWARE. GENERAL ASSEMBLY. HOUSE.
Votes of the House of Assembly of the Delaware State, at a session commenced at Dover, on Monday the fifth day of September, in the year of our Lord, one thousand seven hundred and

ninety-one. Wilmington, Printed by Brynberg and Andrews [1791]. § 11 p.; fol.

Bristol (Evans 46150); Hawkins B:33.
Copies: De; PHi (now in PPL).

292. DELAWARE. GENERAL ASSEMBLY. HOUSE.
Votes and proceedings of the House of Assembly of the Delaware State, at a session commenced at Dover, on Thursday the twentieth day of October, in the year of our Lord one thousand seven hundred and ninety-one. Wilmington, Printed by James Adams, in High-Street, 1791. § 13 p.; fol.

Bristol (Evans 46151); Hawkins B:34.
Copies: De.

293. DELAWARE. LAWS.
Laws of the Delaware State, passed at a session of the General Assembly, commenced at Dover, on the fourth day of January, 1791. Wilmington, Printed by Frederick Craig and Co., 1791. § 37, [1] p.; fol.

Evans 23321.
Copies: DLC; NNB.

294. DELAWARE. LAWS.
Laws of the Delaware State, passed at a session of the General Assembly, commenced at Dover, on the twentieth day of October, 1791. Wilmington, Printed by Brynberg and Andrews [1791]. § 5 p.; fol.

Bristol (Evans 46152); Hawkins B:32.
Copies: NNB.

295. The Delaware gazette. No. 301, Saturday, January 1 [–no. 353, Saturday, December 31, 1791]. Wilmington, Printed and published by Frederick Craig and Co. [and Peter Brynberg and Samuel Andrews, in Market-Street] 1791. § fol.; weekly.

On March 5, 1791, the firm Frederick Craig and Co. was dissolved, and the paper was taken over by Peter Brynberg and Samuel Andrews, cf. Brigham, v. 1, p. 81.

Evans 23323.
Copies: DLC; DeHi (part on microfilm); MH; NN; PHi.

296. DILWORTH, THOMAS, d. 1780.
    A new guide to the English tongue. In five parts, containing words, both common and proper . . . Wilmington, Brynberg and Andrews, 1791. § 142 p.; 12mo.

Bristol (Evans 46158).
Copies: OCl; WHi.

297. DILWORTH, THOMAS, d. 1780.
    The schoolmasters assistant: being a compendium of arithmetic, both practical and theoretical. In five parts . . . Wilmington, Printed and sold by Andrews, Craig, and Brynberg, in Market-Street, 1791. § xiv, [10], 192 p.; fold. table, port.; 12mo.

Evans 23326.
Copies: De(M); DeHi; DeWI; MWA; PHi (now in PPL); PP.

298. EVANS, OLIVER, 1755–1819.
    Improvements on the art of manufacturing grain into flour or meal. [Wilmington? 1791?]. § Broadside; illus.; 52.5 by 43 cm.

Includes two "certificates of the utility of the improvements," dated Aug. 4, 1790, and March 28, 1791.

Bristol (Evans 46164); N.Y. Pub. Libr., 991.
Copies: NN.

299. FOX, THOMAS.
    The Wilmington almanack, or ephemeris, for the year of our Lord, 1792 . . . Wilmington, Printed and sold by James Adams [1791]. § [48] p.; 12mo.

Evans 23382.
Copies: DLC; DeHi; P; PPL.

300. NEW CASTLE CO., DEL.
    Ordinances, rules and bye-laws for the poor-house of New-Castle County . . . Wilmington, Printed by James Adams, 1791. § Broadside; 50 by 40 cm.

Evans 23594.
Copies: DLC; PHi.

301.   Tables of duties, payable on goods, imported into the United
        States of America, after the 31st day of December, 1790, by
act of Congress of the 10th of August, 1790. Also, rates of fees,
coins, and of tonnage, by the Act for the collection of the said duties,
and by the Act for laying a tonnage on vessels . . . Wilmington,
Printed and sold by Peter Brynberg and Samuel Andrews, in Market-Street, 1791.

Evans 23894.
No copy known.

302.   WHARTON, CHARLES HENRY, 1748–1833.
        A short and candid enquiry into the proofs of Christ's divin-
ity; in which Dr. Priestly's [!] History of opinions concerning
Christ is occasionally considered. In a letter to a friend. By Charles
H. Wharton . . . Wilmington, Printed and sold by Brynberg and
Andrews, 1791. § 48 p.; 12mo.

Evans 23995.
Copies: DeHi (photocopy); NHi; PPL.

1792

303.   COLESBERRY, HENRY, d. 1849.
        Tentamen medicum inaugurale de epilepsia. Wilmingtonii,
Apud Brynberg et Andrews, 1792. § 28 p.; 8vo.

Evans 24198.
Copies: DNLM; PHi (now in PPL).

304.   The Columbian almanac; or the North American calendar,
        for the year of our Lord 1793 . . . Wilmington, Printed and
sold by Peter Brynberg and Samuel Andrews in Market-Street
[1792]. § [48] p.; 12mo.

Evans 24202.
Copies: DLC; DeHi; DeWI; MWA; PPL.

305. DELAWARE. CONSTITUTION.
The Constitution of the State of Delaware. Wilmington,
Printed by Brynberg and Andrews in Market Street, 1792. § 42 p.;
8vo.

Evans 24259.
Copies: DLC; DeWI; NN.

306. DELAWARE. CONSTITUTION.
The Constitution of the State of Delaware. Done in Convention, the twelfth day of June, in the year . . . one thousand seven
hundred and ninety-two. Wilmington, Brynberg & Andrews,
printers, 1792. § 86–107 p.; fol.

Probably detached from the *Minutes of the Convention of the Delaware State* . . .

Copies: DLC.

307. DELAWARE. CONSTITUTION.
Draught of a constitution of government: published for the
consideration of the citizens of the Delaware State; pursuant to an
order of the Convention, of the 31st of December, 1791. Wilmington, Printed by Peter Brynberg and Samuel Andrews, in Market-
Street, 1792. § 24 p.; 8vo.

Evans 24257.
Copies: DLC; De(JD); DeGE (photocopy); NN; PPL.

308. DELAWARE. CONSTITUTIONAL CONVENTION, 1791–
1792.
Minutes of the Convention of the Delaware State, which commenced at Dover, on Tuesday the twenty-ninth day of November,
in the year of our Lord one thousand seven hundred and ninety-one,
for the purpose of reviewing, altering, and amending, the constitution of this State, or if they see occasion, for forming a new one instead thereof. Wilmington, Printed by Peter Brynberg and Samuel
Andrews, 1792. § 74 p.; fol.

Bowker, p. 607; Hawkins B:37.
Copies: De; DeHi.

309. DELAWARE. CONSTITUTIONAL CONVENTION, 1791–1792.

Minutes of the Convention of the Delaware State, at the second session thereof, which commenced at Dover, on Tuesday the twenty-ninth day of May, it [!] the year of our Lord, one thousand seven hundred and ninety-two, for the purpose of reviewing, altering, and amending the Constitution of this State, or if they see occasion, for forming a new one instead thereof. Wilmington, Printed by Brynberg and Andrews [1792]. § 107 p.; fol.

Evans 24258.
Copies: De; DeHi; PPL.

310. DELAWARE. CONSTITUTIONAL CONVENTION, 1791–1792.

Minutes of the Grand Committee of the Whole Convention of the Delaware State, which commenced at Dover, on Tuesday, the twenty-ninth day of November, in the year of our Lord one thousand seven hundred and ninety-one, for the purpose of reviewing, altering, and amending the Constitution of this State; or, if they see occasion, for forming a new one instead thereof. Wilmington, Printed by James Adams, in High-Street, 1792. § 80 p.; fol.

Evans 24256.
Copies: De; DeHi; PPL.

311. DELAWARE. GENERAL ASSEMBLY. HOUSE.

Journal of the House of Representatives of the State of Delaware, at a session, commenced at Dover, on Thursday the first day of November, in the year of our Lord one thousand seven hundred and ninety-two. Wilmington, Printed by Brynberg and Andrews [1792]. § 13 p.; 4to.

Bristol (Evans 46427); Hawkins B:35.
Copies: De; DeHi.

312. DELAWARE. GENERAL ASSEMBLY. SENATE.

Journal of the Senate of the State of Delaware, at a session commenced and held at Dover, for the said State, on Thursday the first day of November, in the year of our Lord one thousand seven hundred and ninety-two. Wilmington, Printed by James Adams, in High-Street, 1792. § 9 p.; 4to.

Bristol (Evans 46428); Hawkins B:36.
Copies: DLC; De (photocopy); DeHi.

313. DELAWARE. LAWS.
Laws of the Delaware State, passed at a session of the General Assembly, which commenced at Dover, on the third day of January, 1792. Wilmington, Printed by James Adams, 1792. § 31 p.; fol.

Evans 24255.
Copies: DLC; NNB; PPAmP.

314. The Delaware gazette. No. 354, Saturday, January 7 [–no. 405, Saturday, December 29, 1792]. Wilmington, Printed and sold by Peter Brynberg and Samuel Andrews, in Market-Street, 1792. § fol.; weekly.

Evans 24260.
Copies: DLC; DeHi (part on microfilm); MWA; PHi.

315. DILWORTH, THOMAS, d. 1780.
The schoolmaster's assistant; being a compendium of arithmetic, both practical and theoretical. In five parts . . . The whole being delivered in the most familiar way of question and answer. Wilmington, Printed by Brynberg and Andrews, in Market Street, 1792. § port.; 12mo.

Evans 24270.
No copy known.

316. EDWARDS, JONATHAN, 1703–1758.
An humble inquiry into the rules of the word of God, concerning the qualifications requisite to a complete standing and full communion in the visible Christian church . . . Wilmington, Printed by James Adams, sen., 1792.

Evans 24289.
No copy known.

317. [ELIOT, JOSEPH] 1638–1694.
The life of faith exemplified and recommended: in a letter found in the study of the Rev. Mr. Blair, late of Doninham, New-ingham. Being an answer to this question—How to live in this world, so as to live in Heaven. Wilmington, Printed and sold by James Adams, 1792.

Attributed by Samuel A. Green to Joseph Eliot, cf. Proceedings of the Mass. Hist. Soc., vol. 18, 1904, p. 468ff. The title of other known editions reads in part: "in a letter found in the study of the Rev. Mr. Joseph Belcher, late of Dedham in New-England."

Evans 24117 (entry under Blair).
No copy known.

318. FOX, THOMAS.
The Wilmington almanack, or ephemeris, for the year of our Lord 1793. Wilmington [1792].

Evans 24329.
No copy known.

319. LONDON. CHURCH OF CHRIST.
A declaration of the faith and practice of the Church of Christ in Carter Lane, Southwark, London, under the pastoral care of Dr. John Gill; read and assented to at the admission of members. Wilmington, Printed and sold by James Adams, 1792.

Evans 24481.
No copy known.

320. LOVE, CHRISTOPHER, 1618–1651.
Sixteen sermons; wherein is plainly shewn true grace, with its different degrees;—and several important cases of conscience answered in the course of the work. By the worthy and eminently pious Christopher Love, minister of the Gospel, in Laurence-Jury, London;—who was beheaded on Tower-Hill, in the time of Crom-well's usurpation, being the last he preached . . . Wilmington, Printed and sold by James Adams, 1792. § 244 p.; 12mo.

Evans 24482.
Copies: DLC; DeHi; DeWI; MWA; NN; PHi (now in PPL); PPPrHi.

321.   NEW CASTLE CO., DEL. COURT OF COMMON PLEAS.
Causes for argument and trial, before the Honourable the
Court of Common-Pleas, to be held at New-Castle, for the County
of New-Castle, at the November term, A.D. one thousand seven
hundred and ninety-two . . . [Wilmington] 1792. § Broadside;
41 by 30 cm.

Dated: October 26, 1792.

Copies: DeHi.

322.   A sermon on Luke, xix.10. Wilmington, Printed by Bryn-
       berg and Andrews, in Market-Street, 1792. § [24] p.; 12mo.

Signed: P.H.

Evans 25575.
Copies: DeHi.

323.   A small sketch on natural philosophy. Wilmington, Printed
       by Brynberg and Andrews, in Market-Street, 1792. § [24] p.;
12mo.

Signed: P.H.

Evans 25576.
Copies: DeHi.

324.   [SMITH, ELIAS] 1769–1846.
An essay on the fall of angels and men; with remarks on
Dr. Edward's notion of the freedom of the will, and the system of
universality. Wilmington, Printed by Brynberg and Andrews, in
Market-Street, 1792. § iv, 76 p.; 12mo.

Signed: E.S.

Evans 26169.
Copies: DLC; DeHi.

325.   SWEETING, WHITING, d. 1791.
The narrative of Whiting Sweeting, who was executed an
[!] Albany thr [!] 26th of August, 1791. Containing, an account of
his trial before the Supreme Court of Judicature of the State of New-

York, at the July term, 1791, for the murder of Darius Quimby, the substance of the charge of His Honour the Chief-Justice to the jury, with the sentence of death on the prisoner. An address to the public on the fatal consequences of a life spent in sin, instanced in his own conduct setting forth the great necessity of remembering our Creator in the days of our youth, and practising religion and virtue in our whole lives. With an address to his parents, brothers and sisters, wife and children, and many others; also a brief account of him, by William Carter, from his first confinement till the time of execution. Wilmington, Printed and sold by Peter Brynberg and Samuel Andrews in Market-Street, 1792.

Evans 24837.
No copy known.

1793

326.   BIBLE. O.T. PSALMS.
        Psalms carefully suited to the Christian worship in the United States of America, being an improvement of the old versions of the Psalms of David. Adapted to the state of the Christian church in general. To this edition are added the words of sundry anthems . . . Wilmington, Printed by Brynberg and Andrews, in Market-Street, 1793. § 315 p.; 12mo.

Bristol (Evans 46699).
Copies: DeWI; MWA.

327.   The Columbian almanac; or, The North American calendar, for the year of our Lord 1794 . . . Wilmington, Printed and sold by Peter Brynberg and Samuel Andrews, in Market-Street [1793]. § [48] p.; 12mo.

Evans 25316.
Copies: DLC; DeHi; DeWI; DeWin; MWA; NHi; PHi (now in PPL).

328.   DELAWARE. GENERAL ASSEMBLY. HOUSE.
        Journal of the House of Representatives of the State of Delaware, at a session commenced at Dover, on Tuesday, the first day

of January, in the year of our Lord one thousand seven hundred and ninety-three. Wilmington, Printed at Adams's Press, 1793. § 82 p.; 4to.

Bristol (Evans 46725); Hawkins B:38.
Copies: De; DeHi; DeWI.

329. DELAWARE. GENERAL ASSEMBLY. HOUSE.
Journal of the House of Representatives of the State of Delaware, at a session commenced at Dover, on Monday, the twenty-seventh day of May, in the year of our Lord one thousand seven hundred and ninety-three. Wilmington, Printed by Samuel and John Adams, at the corner of King and High-Streets, 1793. § 55 p.; 4to.

Bristol (Evans 46726); Hawkins B:39.
Copies: De; DeHi.

330. DELAWARE. GENERAL ASSEMBLY. SENATE.
Journal of the Senate of the State of Delaware, at a session commenced and held at Dover, for the said State, on Tuesday, the first day of January, in the year of our Lord one thousand seven hundred and ninety-three. Wilmington, Done at Adams's Press, 1793. § 41 p.; 4to.

Bristol (Evans 46727); Hawkins B:40.
Copies: DLC; De; DeHi.

331. DELAWARE. GENERAL ASSEMBLY. SENATE.
Journal of the Senate of the State of Delaware, at a session of the Legislature, commenced and held at Dover, on Monday the twenty-seventh day of May, in the year of our Lord one thousand seven hundred and ninety-three . . . Wilmington, Printed by Samuel and John Adams, at the corner of King and High-Streets, 1793. § 40 p.; 4to.

Bristol (Evans 46728); Hawkins B:41.
Copies: DLC; De; DeHi.

332. DELAWARE. LAWS.
An act for establishing the militia of the State of Delaware . . . Wilmington, Printed by Brynberg and Andrews [1793]. § 21 p.; 4to.

Passed at Dover, June 18, 1793.
Copies: DeWI.

333.   DELAWARE. LAWS.
Laws of the State of Delaware. Published by authority. Wilmington, Printed by Peter Brynberg and Samuel Andrews, in Market-Street, 1793. § 91 p.; 8vo.
Evans 25387.
Copies: DLC; PPAmP.

334.   DELAWARE. LAWS.
Laws of the State of Delaware. Published by authority. Wilmington, Printed by Peter Brynberg and Samuel Andrews, in Market-Street, 1793. § [2], [93]–263, [1] p.; 8vo.
Evans 25388.
Copies: DLC; De; PPAmP.

335.   The Delaware gazette. No. 406, Saturday, January 5 [–no.
457, Saturday, December 28, 1793]. Wilmington, Printed and sold by Peter Brynberg and Samuel Andrews, in Market-Street, 1793. § fol.; weekly.
Evans 25389.
Copies: DLC; DeHi; DeU; MWA; PHi.

336.   FOX, THOMAS.
The Wilmington almanac, or ephemeris, for the year of our Lord 1794 . . . Wilmington, Printed and sold by Samuel and John Adams [1793]. § [36] p.; 12mo.
Evans 25494.
Copies: DLC; DeHi; MdHi; MWA.

337.   GOODY TWO SHOES.
The history of little Goody Two-Shoes, otherwise called Mrs. Margery Two-Shoes . . . Wilmington, Printed by Brynberg and Andrews, 1793. § 127 p.; illus.; 16mo.

Variously attributed to Oliver Goldsmith, Giles Jones and others.

Bristol (Evans 46764).
Copies: DeWI.

338. NELSON, ROBERT, 1656–1715.
Instructions necessary and useful for those who are to be confirmed; in the way of questions and answers, with prayers suitable to the occasion . . . First American ed. from the twenty-seventh London ed. Wilmington, Printed by Samuel and John Adams, at the corner of King and High-Streets, 1793. § 24 p.; 12mo.

Copies: CtY; PPM (inactive; collections dispersed).

339. SPURRIER, JOHN.
The practical farmer: being a new and compendious system of husbandry, adapted to the different soils and climates of America. Containing the mechanical, chemical and philosophical elements of agriculture. With many other useful and interesting subjects . . . Wilmington, Printed by Brynberg and Andrews, 1793. § [2], x, [iii]–x, [11]–360, xv p.; 8vo.

Evans 26198.
Copies: DLC; De(M); DeGE; DeHi; DeWI; DeWin; MWA; NN; PPL; PU.

340. WATTS, ISAAC, 1674–1748.
Hymns and spiritual songs. In three books. I. Collected from the Scriptures. II. Composed on divine subjects. III. Prepared for the Lord's Supper . . . Wilmington, Printed by Brynberg and Andrews, in Market-Street, 1793. § 284 p.; 32mo.

Bristol (Evans 46936).
Copies: DeWI; PSC.

341. ZANCHI, GIROLAMO, 1516–1590.
The doctrine of absolute predestination stated and asserted: with a preliminary discourse on the divine attributes. Translated, in great measure, from the Latin of Jerom Zanchius. By Augustus Toplady . . . Wilmington, Printed at Adams's Press, 1793. § xii, 13–148 p.; 12mo.

Evans 26526.
Copies: CSmH; DLC; DeGE; DeWI; MWA; PHi (now in PPL); PU; RPJCB.

342. BANNEKER, BENJAMIN, 1731–1806.
Bannaker's [!] New Jersey, Pennsylvania, Delaware, Maryland, and Virginia almanac, or ephemeris, for the year of our Lord 1795 . . . Wilmington, Printed by S. & J. Adams [1794]. § [36] p.; port.; 12mo.

Bristol, p. 492; Drake 1393, 1394.
Copies: DLC; DeWI; NHi.

343. BANNEKER, BENJAMIN, 1731–1806.
Bannaker's [!] Wilmington almanac, or ephemeris, for the year of our Lord 1795 . . . Wilmington, Printed by S. & J. Adams for Frederick Craig [1794]. § [36] p.; 12mo.

Drake 1396.
Copies: DeHi; MWA; OCHP.

344. BANNEKER, BENJAMIN, 1731–1806.
Bannaker's [!] Wilmington almanac, or ephemeris, for the year of our Lord 1795 . . . Wilmington, Printed by S. & J. Adams, sold by W. C. Smyth [1794]. § 36 p.; 12mo.

Drake 1395, 1397; Evans 26613.
Copies: DeWin; MdBP.

345. BANNEKER, BENJAMIN, 1731–1806.
Benjamin Banneker's Pennsylvania, Delaware, Maryland, and Virginia almanac, for the year of our Lord, 1795 . . . Wilmington, Printed and sold by S. & J. Adams [1794]. § [36?] p.; port.; 12mo.

Drake 1398; Evans 26612.
No copy known.

346. BIBLE. N.T.
The New Testament of our Lord and Saviour Jesus Christ, newly translated out of the original Greek; and with the former translations diligently compared and revised. Wilmington, Printed and sold by Peter Brynberg and Samuel Andrews in Market-Street [1794?]. § [302] p.; 8vo.

Bristol (Evans 46983); Hawkins B:42.
Copies: DeWI; Privately held by Mr. James F. Walker, Wilmington.

347.   CARRÉ, C.
       Tableau de son & accens de la langue anglaise. Wilmington, De l'imprimerie de S. & J. Adams, 1794.

Evans 26743.
No copy known.

348.   The Columbian almanac; or, The North American calendar, for the year of our Lord 1795 . . . Wilmington, Printed and sold by Peter Brynberg and Samuel Andrews, in Market-Street [1794].
§ [36] p.; 12mo.

Evans 26786.
Copies: DeWI; PHi (now in PPL).

349.   DELAWARE. GENERAL ASSEMBLY. HOUSE
       Journal of the House of Representatives of Delaware. Wilmington, Printed by S. & J. Adams, 1794.

Evans 28556.
No copy known.

350.   DELAWARE. GENERAL ASSEMBLY. HOUSE.
       Journal of the House of Representatives of the State of Delaware at a session commenced at Dover, on Tuesday the seventh day of January, in the year of our Lord, one thousand seven hundred and ninety-four. Wilmington, Printed by Peter Brynberg and Samuel Andrews, 1794. § [101] p. incl. 3 fold. tables; 4to.

Hawkins B:43.
Copies: De; DeHi.

351.   DELAWARE. GENERAL ASSEMBLY. SENATE.
       Journal of the Senate of the State of Delaware, at a session commenced and held at Dover, for the said State, on Tuesday the seventeenth [i.e. seventh] day of January, in the year of our Lord one thousand seven hundred and ninety-four. Wilmington, Printed by Samuel and John Adams, 1794. § 78 p.; 3 fold. tables; 4to.

Evans 26867.
Copies: DLC; De; DeHi.

352. DELAWARE. LAWS.

Laws of the State of Delaware, passed at a session of the General Assembly, which was begun and held at Dover on Tuesday, the seventh day of January, and ended on Saturday, the eighth day of February, in the year of our Lord, one thousand seven hundred and ninety-four . . . Published by authority. Wilmington, Printed by Brynberg and Andrews, 1794. § [265]–314, [1] p.; 8vo.

Evans 26868.
Copies: DLC; De(JD); NHi; PHi; PPAmP.

353. DELAWARE. MILITIA.

Attention, Light Infantry. Saturday 20th inst. being appointed as a field day for the First Regiment of Delaware Militia, on which occasion a full and punctual attendance on the ground near the ferry, at 11 o'clock, A.M. is particularly requested . . . Wilmington, Printed by Brynberg and Andrews [1794]. § Broadside; 25.5 by 18 cm.

Signed: David Bush, Capt. Wilmington, September 13th, 1794.

Bristol (Evans 47030).
Copies: PHi.

354. The Delaware and Eastern-Shore advertiser. No. 1, Wednesday, May 14 [–no. 67, Wednesday, December 31, 1794]. Wilmington, Printed by S. & J. Adams & W. C. Smyth, corner of King and High-Streets, 1794. § fol.; semi-weekly.

Evans 26869.
Copies: DeHi (part on microfilm); DeU (microfilm); PHi.

355. The Delaware gazette. No. 458, Saturday, January 4 [–no. 509, Saturday, December 27, 1794]. Wilmington, Printed and sold by Peter Brynberg and Samuel Andrews, in Market-Street, 1794. § fol.; weekly.

Evans 26870.
Copies: DeHi; MWA; PHi.

356. DILWORTH, THOMAS, d. 1780.
[A new guide to the English tongue]. Wilmington, Brynberg & Andrews, 1794. § 140, [2] p.; illus.; 12mo.

Copies: DeHi (imperfect; most of title page missing).

357. [KEATE, GEORGE] 1729–1797.
An account of the Pelew Islands, situated in the great South Sea. Composed from the journals of Capt. Henry Wilson, and his officers; who, in August, 1783, were there shipwrecked in the Antelope packet . . . Wilmington, Printed for the Rev. M. L. Weems, by Samuel and John Adams, corner of King and High-Streets, 1794. § iv, 96 p.; 12mo.
Evans 27177.
Copies: DLC; DeU; DeWI; MWA; NN; PPL; RPJCB.

358. MARMONTEL, JEAN FRANÇOIS, 1723–1799.
The shepherdess of the Alps. A moral tale. Translated from the French of Monsieur Marmontell[!]. By Evan Thomas. Wilmington, Printed by Brynberg and Andrews, 1794. § 86 p.; 12mo.
Evans 29021.
Copies: DeHi; DeWI.

359. The New-England primer, with the shorter catechism. Wilmington, Printed by Brynberg & Andrews, 1794. § 72 p.; 16mo.
Bristol (Evans 47123).
Copies: Mrs. A. Ward France, Wyncote, Pa.

360. PATRIOTIC SOCIETY OF NEW CASTLE COUNTY.
The address of the Patriotic Society of Newcastle County, in the State of Delaware, to the people of the United States of America. Wilmington, January 8, 1794. § Broadside; 53 by 41 cm.

Signed: James M'Cullough, President; Attest. J. Bird, Secretary.

Copies: DeHi.

361. PATRIOTIC SOCIETY OF NEW CASTLE COUNTY.
Declaration of the political principles of the Patriotic Society of New Castle County in the State of Delaware. Constitution of the

Patriotic Society. James McCulloch [!], president, J. Bird, attest. New Castle, Aug. 30, 1794. Wilmington, Printed by Adams and Smyth, 1794. § 12 p.; 8vo.

Copies: DeHi.

362. Reflections on taxes: the principles whereof are essentially applicable to Republican government. By a landholder. Wilmington, Printed by S. & J. Adams, 1794.

Evans 27601 (from adv. in *Delaware and Eastern-Shore advertiser*, May 31, 1794).
No copy known.

363. U.S. INSPECTOR-GENERAL'S OFFICE.
Regulations for the order and discipline of the volunteer army of the United States of America, agreeable to Baron Steuban [!]. With instructions for the exercise of the light horse. Wilmington, Printed by S. & J. Adams, 1794.

Possibly mistaken for another edition, issued in Baltimore with the imprint: Printed by S. & J. Adams for George Keatinge, 1794. A copy of this edition is at PPAmP.

Evans 27973 (from adv. in *Delaware and Eastern-Shore advertiser*, Nov. 15, 1794).
No copy known.

364. WILCOX, THOMAS, 1622–1687.
A choice drop of honey from the rock Christ; or, A short word of advice to all saints and sinners; whereby they may be helped to stand upon the right foundation lest they fall; and great be their fall. By Thomas Wilcox. Wilmington, Printed by S. & J. Adams, 1794.

Evans 28085 (from adv. in *Delaware and Eastern-Shore advertiser*, May 3, 1794).
No copy known.

365.   AUSTIN, DAVID, 1760–1831.

The millenium; or, The thousand years of prosperity, promised to the Church of God, in the Old and New Testament, shortly
to be carried on to perfection. Wilmington, Printed and sold at
James Adams's printing-office, opposite the upper Market-House,
1795.

Evans 28220 (from adv. in *Delaware and Eastern-Shore advertiser*,
Jan. 14, 1795).
No copy known.

366.   [BROTHERS, RICHARD] 1757–1824.

A revealed knowledge of the prophecies and times, particularly of the present time, the present war, and the prophecy now
fulfilling. Containing, with other great and remarkable things, not
revealed to any other person on earth, the sudden and perpetual fall
of the Turkish, German and Russian empires . . . By the Man that
will be revealed to the Hebrews as their prince and prophet. In the
year of the world 5913. Wilmington, Printed by S. & J. Adams,
1795.

Evans 28360.
No copy known.

367.   The Columbian almanac; or, The North-American calendar,
for the year of our Lord 1796 . . . Wilmington, Printed and
sold by Peter Brynberg, and Samuel Andrews, in Market-Street
[1795]. § [36] p.; 12mo.

Evans 28450.
Copies: DLC; DeWI; DeWin; MWA; NHi; OCHP; PHi.

368.   DELAWARE. GENERAL ASSEMBLY. HOUSE.

Journal of the House of Representatives of the State of Delaware, at a session commenced at Dover, on Tuesday the sixth day
of January, in the year of our Lord one thousand seven hundred and
ninety-five. Wilmington, Printed by Samuel and John Adams, in
High-Street, 1795. § 92 p.; 4to.

Evans 28557.
Copies: De; DeHi.

369. DELAWARE. GENERAL ASSEMBLY. SENATE.
Journal of the Senate of the State of Delaware, at a session commenced at Dover, on Tuesday, the sixth day of January, in the year of our Lord one thousand seven hundred and ninety-five . . . Wilmington, Printed by Samuel and John Adams, 1795. § 68 p.; 9 fold. tables; 4to.

Evans 28558.
Copies: DLC; De; DeHi.

370. DELAWARE. LAWS.
Laws of the State of Delaware, passed at a session of the General Assembly, which was begun and held at Dover, on Tuesday, the sixth day of January, in the year of our Lord one thousand seven hundred and ninety-five . . . Published by authority. Wilmington, Printed by Brynberg & Andrews, 1795. § [2], 319–356, [1] p.; 8vo.

Evans 28559.
Copies: DLC; PPAmP.

371. The Delaware and Eastern-Shore advertiser. No. 68, Saturday, January 3 [–no. 171, Wednesday, December 30, 1795]. Wilmington, Printed by Sam. & John Adams, & W. C. Smyth, corner of King & High-Streets, 1795. § fol.; semi-weekly.

Evans 28560.
Copies: DeHi (part on microfilm); DeU (microfilm); PHi; PPL.

372. The Delaware gazette. No. 510, Saturday, January 3 [–no. 578, Tuesday, December 29, 1795]. Wilmington, Printed & sold by Peter Brynberg & Samuel Andrews, in Market Street, 1795. § fol.; weekly; semi-weekly from September 11.

Imprint beginning September 8: Printed for Robert Coram, by Bonsal & Starr, in Market-Street.
Evans 28561.
Copies: DLC; DeHi; MH; MWA; PPL.

373. DUKE, WILLIAM, 1757–1840.
A clew to religious truth, obviating the more common suggestions of infidelity, and leading the serious inquirer into such an

acquaintance with Christianity as may avail to the saving of his soul . . . Wilmington, Printed by Samuel and John Adams, 1795. § xii, 13–374 p., 1l.; 12mo.

Evans 28592.
Copies: CSmH; DeHi; DeU; DeWI; MWA; MdBP; MdHi; NN; PHi (now in PPL); RPJCB.

374. [ERRA PATER?]
The universal interpreter of dreams and visions. Part I. Shewing the nature, causes and uses of various kinds of dreams and representations . . . Part II. Shewing the signification of all manner of dreams, alphabetically arranged . . . Baltimore, Printed for Keatinge's book-store, 1795. § iv, [5]–208 p.; 12mo.

Part II has title: Part II. The universal dream-dictionary. Wilmington, Printed by Bonsal & Starr, for Keatinge's book-store, Baltimore, 1795.

Evans 28635.
Copies: NN.

375. FOX, THOMAS.
United States almanac, and ephemeris for 1796. Wilmington, J. Adams and H. Niles [1795]. § [40] p.

Drake 1401.
Copies: PHi? (copy not located).

376. GRUBB, SARAH (TUKE) 1756–1790.
Some account of the life and religious labours of Sarah Grubb. With an appendix, containing an account of the schools at Ackworth and York, observations on Christian discipline, and extracts from many of her letters . . . Wilmington, Printed by V. Bonsal & C. Starr, 1795. § v, [6]–378, [1] p.; 12mo.

Evans 28777.
Copies: DLC; DeGE; DeHi; DeU; DeWI; DeWin; IU; KyLx; MH; MWA; NHi; PHi (now in PPL); PSC-Hi.

377. HELME, ELIZABETH, d. 1816.
The history of Louisa, the lovely orphan; or The cottage on the moor . . . By Mrs. Helme. The eighth edition. Wilmington,

Printed for the Rev. M. L. Weems, by Samuel and John Adams, corner of King and High-Streets, 1795. § 2 v. in 1 (153 p.); 3 plates; 12mo.

Evans 28819.

Copies: CSmH; DeWI; MWA; NN.

378. PEIRCE, JOHN.
The new American spelling-book: in three parts. Containing, I. Dilworth's Tables of common words . . . II. A collection of words of two, three, and four syllables . . . III. A very plain and easy introduction to English grammar . . . Compiled by John Peirce, jun. The seventh edition. Wilmington, Printed and sold by Brynberg and Andrews, in Market-Street, 1795. § iv, [2], 198 p.; 12mo.

Copies: DeWI.

379. PROTESTANT EPISCOPAL CHURCH IN THE U.S.A. DELAWARE (DIOCESE).
Journal of the proceedings of the Second Convention of the Protestant Episcopal Church in the State of Delaware, held in Dover, on Tuesday, the eighteenth day of December, 1792. Wilmington, Printed by Brynberg and Andrews, in Market Street, 1795. § 8 p.; 8vo.

Copies: DeWE; DeWI (undated reprint); TxAuC.

380. PROTESTANT EPISCOPAL CHURCH IN THE U.S.A. DELAWARE (DIOCESE).
Journal of the proceedings of the Fourth Convention of the Protestant Episcopal Church in the State of Delaware, held in Dover, on Tuesday, the sixteenth day of December, 1794. Wilmington, Printed by Brynberg and Andrews, in Market-Street, 1795. § 8 p.; 8vo.

Copies: DeWE; DeWI (undated reprint).

381. PROTESTANT EPISCOPAL CHURCH IN THE U.S.A. DELAWARE (DIOCESE).
Journal of the proceedings of the Fifth Convention of the Protestant Episcopal Church in the State of Delaware, held in Dover, on

Tuesday, the fifth day of May, 1795. Wilmington, Printed by Peter Brynberg [1795?]. § 5 p.; 8vo.

Copies: DeWE; DeWI (undated reprint); MCE.

382. U.S. Inspector-General's Office.
Regulations for the order and discipline of the volunteer army of the United States of America, agreeable to Baron Steuben; with instructions for the exercise of the light horse. Wilmington, Printed by Samuel and John Adams, 1795.

Evans 29779.
No copy known.

383. U.S. Treaties.
Treaty of amity, commerce and navigation between His Britannic Majesty, and the United States of America. Wilmington, Printed by Bonsal & Starr, 1795.

Evans 29751 (from adv. in *Delaware gazette*, Aug. 15, 1795).
No copy known.

384. Wilmer, James Jones, 1749–1814.
Support under trials . . . Wilmington, Printed for the author by Samuel and John Adams [1795]. § 48 p.; 12mo.

Evans 29903.
Copies: DLC; PPL.

1796

385. [Bacon, Nathaniel] 1593–1660.
A relation of the fearful state of Francis Spira, after he turned apostate from the protestant church to popery. To which is added an account of the miserable lives and woful [!] deaths of Mr. John Child, who hung himself in Brick-Lane, Spittle-Fields, London, 1684; and Mr. George Edwards who shot himself, Jan. 4, 1704. Also, the remarkable history of John Diazius . . . Wilmington, Printed by P. Brynberg, for J. Thompson [1796]. § 57 p.; 8vo.

Evans 30012.
Copies: DLC; DeWI; PHi.

386. [BERQUIN, ARNAUD] 1747–1791.
     The blossoms of morality; intended for the amusement and
instruction of young ladies and gentlemen. By the editor of the
Looking-glass for the mind. Second American edition. Wilmington, Printed by Joseph Johnson & Co., No. 73 Market-Street,
1796. § 184 p.; 8vo.

Evans 30277 (assigns to Samuel Cooper).
Copies: CSmH; DLC; DeWI; DeWin; MWA; NN.

387. BERQUIN, ARNAUD, 1747–1791.
     The children's friend and youth's monitor. Consisting of
tales and stories, equally adapted for instruction and entertainment.
Translated from the French of M. Berquin . . . Wilmington, Printed by Joseph Johnson, in Market-Street, opposite the bank, 1796.
§ [2], 108 p.; 12mo.

Bristol (Evans 47721).
Copies: MWA.

388. BIBLE. O.T. PSALMS.
     The whole book of Psalms in metre; with hymns suited to
the feasts and fasts of the church, and other occasions. Wilmington, Printed by Peter Brynberg [1796]. § [2], 226, [2] p.; 12mo.

Evans 30079 (from adv. in no. 391).
No copy known.

389. BRACKEN, HENRY, 1679–1764.
     Bracken's farriery abridg'd; or, The gentleman's pocket far-
rier; showing how to use your horse on a journey; and what treat-
ments are proper for common accidents, that may befall him on the
road . . . Wilmington, Printed by J. Wilson, book-binder, bookseller and stationer, 1796. § 64 p.; 16mo.

Copies: DeWin.

390. The Columbian almanac; or, The North-American calendar,
for the year of our Lord 1797 . . . Wilmington, Printed and sold by
Peter Brynberg, in Market-Street [1796]. § [36] p.; 12mo.

Evans 30246.
Copies: DeWI; MWA; N.

391. CORREY, MOLLESTON.
The travelling millennarian, to the people of America . . .
Wilmington, Printed by Bonsal & Niles, for Molleston Correy,
the author [1796?]. § 60 p.; 8vo.

Reed 972.
Copies: DeU.

392. DEFOE, DANIEL, 1661?–1731.
The life and most surprizing adventures of Robinson Crusoe, of York, mariner. Containing a full and particular account how
he lived twenty eight years in an uninhabited island on the coast of
America . . . Faithfully epitomized from the three volumes. Wilmington, Printed & sold by Peter Brynberg, 1796. § iv, 144 p.;
12mo.

Evans 30325.
Copies: DeHi; MWA.

393. DEFOE, DANIEL, 1661?–1731.
The life and most surprizing adventures of Robinson Crusoe, of York, mariner. Containing a full and particular account how
he lived twenty eight years in an uninhabited island on the coast of
America . . . Faithfully epitomized from the three volumes. Wilmington, Printed for, and sold, by James Wilson, bookseller,
binder, & stationer, opposite the Upper Market, 1796. § iv, 144 p.;
12mo.

Copies: DeWin.

394. [DEFOE, DANIEL] 1661?–1731.
Religious courtship: being historical discourses on the necessity of marrying religious husbands and wives only: as also, of
husbands ane [!] wives being of the same opinions with one another. With an appendix: shewing the necessity of taking none but
religious servants; and a preposal [!] for the better managing of
servants. Wilmington, Printed by Joseph Johnson, Market-Street,
opposite the bank, 1796. § v, [7]–303 p.; 12mo.

Evans 30326.
Copies: DeHi; DeU; DeWI; MWA; PHi (now in PPL).

395. DELAWARE. GENERAL ASSEMBLY. HOUSE.

Journal of the House of Representatives of the State of Delaware, at a session commenced at Dover, on Tuesday, the fifth day of January, in the year of our Lord one thousand seven hundred and ninety-six . . . Wilmington, Printed by Samuel and John Adams, 1796. § 147 p.; 8 fold. tables; 4to.

Evans 30327; Hawkins B:54.
Copies: DLC; De; DeHi; DeWI.

396. DELAWARE. GENERAL ASSEMBLY. HOUSE.

Journal of the House of Representatives of the State of Delaware, at a session, commenced at Dover, on Wednesday the ninth day of November, in the year of our Lord one thousand seven hundred and ninety-six . . . Wilmington, Printed by Samuel and John Adams, 1796. § 13 p.; 4to.

Bristol, p. 544 (included in Evans 30327); Hawkins B:55.
Copies: De; DeHi; NN.

397. DELAWARE. GENERAL ASSEMBLY. SENATE.

Journal of the Senate of the State of Delaware, at a session of the Legislature, commenced and held at Dover, on Tuesday, the fifth day of January, in the year of our Lord one thousand seven hundred and ninety-six . . . Wilmington, Printed by Samuel and John Adams, 1796. § 82, [9], 10 p.; 8 fold. tables; 4to.

Evans 30328; Hawkins B:56.
Copies: De; DeHi.

398. DELAWARE. LAWS.

Laws of the State of Delaware, passed at a session of the General Assembly, which was begun and held at Dover, on Tuesday, the fifth day of January, and ended on Wednesday, the tenth day of February, in the year of our Lord one thousand seven hundred and ninety-six . . . Wilmington, Printed by Brynberg and Andrews, 1796. § 1 p.l., 361–496 p., 1 l.; 4to.

Hawkins B:57.
Copies: DeHi; NHi; PPAmP.

399. DELAWARE. LAWS.

Poor laws of the State of Delaware. New-Castle, Printed by Samuel and John Adams, 1796. § 28 p.; 8vo.

"An act for the relief of the poor [passed March 29, 1775]": p. [3]–15.

"An act for the better relief of the poor [passed January 29, 1791]"; "A supplementary act, to an act, intitled: An act for the better relief of the poor . . . [passed February 4, 1792]": p. 15–28.

Evans 30329.
Copies: CSmH; DLC.

400. DELAWARE. LAWS.

A supplement to an act entitled "An act for establishing the militia of the State of Delaware" . . . Wilmington, Printed by Brynberg and Andrews [1796]. § 17 p.; 4to.

Passed February 9, 1796; certified by James Booth, Secretary of the State of Delaware, New-Castle, March 1, 1796.

Copies: DeWI.

401. The Delaware and Eastern-Shore advertiser. No. 172, Saturday, January 2 [–no. 275, Thursday, December 29, 1796]. Wilmington, Printed by Samuel and John Adams, corner of King and High-Streets, 1796. § fol.; semi-weekly.

Evans 30331.
Copies: DeHi; DeU (microfilm); DeWI; MH; MWA; PPL.

402. The Delaware gazette. No. 579, Friday, January 1 [–no. 692, Saturday, December 31, 1796]. Wilmington, Printed for Robert Coram, by Bonsal & Starr, in Market-Street, 1796. § fol.; semi-weekly.

Beginning October 29 issued by: W. C. Smyth, rear of the new fire-engine, Shipley-Street, opposite Capt. O'Flinn's tavern.

Evans 30332.
Copies: DLC; DeHi (part on microfilm); MH; PPL.

403. DILWORTH, THOMAS, d. 1780.
The schoolmasters assistant: being a compendium of arithmetic, both practical and theoretical. In five parts . . . Wilmington, Printed and sold by Peter Brynberg, 1796. § [6], 192 p., 1l.; fold. table, port.; 12mo.

Evans 30352.
Copies: DAU; DLC; DeHi; DeU; DeWI; DeWin; MWA; NN; PPL.

404. FOX, THOMAS.
The United States almanac, and ephemeris, for the year 1797 . . . Wilmington, Printed and sold wholesale and retail by J. Adams and H. Niles, northside of the Upper Market [1796]. § [36] p.; 12mo.

Evans 30437.
Copies: DeHi; DeWI; PHi (now in PPL).

405. GOOCH, ELIZABETH SARAH (VILLA-REAL) b. 1754?
The contrast. A novel. By E. S. Villa-Real Gooch. The first American edition. Wilmington, Printed and sold by Joseph Johnson, No. 73 Market-Street opposite the bank, 1796. § 156 p.; 12mo.

Evans 30497.
Copies: CSmH; CU; CtHT; CtY; DeU; DeWI; DeWin; MWA.

406. GOOCH, ELIZABETH SARAH (VILLA-REAL) b. 1754?
The contrast: a novel. By E. S. Villa-Real Gooch. The first American edition. Wilmington, Printed for and sold by James Wilson, No. 5 opposite the Upper Market, 1796. § 156 p.; 12mo.

Evans 30498.
Copies: CSmH; DLC; DeHi; MWA; NN.

407. GOODY TWO SHOES.
The history of little Goody Two-Shoes. Otherwise called Mrs. Margery Two-Shoes. With the means by which she acquired her learning and wisdom, and in consequence thereof her estate. Set forth at large for the benefit of all those pretty boys and girls

. . . Wilmington, Printed by Peter Brynberg, 1796. § 127 p.; front., illus.; 16mo.

Variously attributed to Oliver Goldsmith, Giles Jones and others.

Evans 32257.
Copies: DeWin; MWA; PHi (now in PPL); PP.

408.   HERVEY, JAMES, 1714–1758.
    The beauties of Hervey: or Descriptive, picturesque and instructive passages, selected from the works of this deservedly admired author . . . to which are added, memoirs of the author's life and character; with an elegiac poem on his death . . . Wilmington, printed for Robert Campbell, Philadelphia, by V. Bonsal, 1796. § xi, [13]–226, [6] p.; 12mo.

Evans 30558.
Copies: DeU; DeWI; DeWin; MWA; NN; RPJCB.

409.   HERVEY, JAMES, 1714–1758.
    Meditations and contemplations among the tombs . . . Wilmington, Printed by Peter Brynberg, for John Boggs, Minister of the Gospel, 1796. § iv, [5]–62, [lxiii]–lxxii p.; 12mo.

Bristol (Evans 47803); Hawkins B:65.
Copies: DeHi; DeWI; DeWin; NN; PHi (now in PPL).

410.   HUGHLETT, WILLIAM.
    Delaware State Mills. [Sir] Being desirous of driving my mills to the extent, it requires a great deal of wheat, corn and rye, to keep them in operation . . . [Wilmington? 1796]. § Broadside; 24 by 16 cm.

Signed: (in autograph) Wm. Hughlett, February 18th 1796.

Bristol (Evans 47806).
Copies: PPL.

411.   Know all men by these presents, that we are held and firmly bound unto Maxwell Bines, Esq. High Sheriff of the aforesaid county of New Castle——. Dated the——day of——in the year of our Lord one thousand seven hundred and ninety——. Newcastle, Printed by S. & J. Adams [1796?]. § Broadside; 32 by 22 cm.

Hawkins C:17.
Copies: DeHi.

412. MacGowan, John, 1726–1780.
    The life of Joseph, the son of Israel. In eight books. Chiefly
designed to allure young minds to a love of the sacred Scriptures.
By John Maggowan [!]. The fifth edition. Wilmington, Printed by
Joseph Johnson, Market-Street, opposite the bank, 1796. § xi,
[13]–173 p.; 12mo.

Evans 30721.
Copies: DeWI; KyLx; MWA; PP.

413. The new Federal primer, or, An easy and pleasant guide to
      the art of reading . . . Wilmington, Printed by Brynberg &
Andrews, 1796. § 72 p.; illus.; 16mo.

Bristol (Evans 47845).
Copies: NN.

414. Protestant Episcopal Church in the U.S.A. Del-
      aware (Diocese).
Journal of the proceedings of the Sixth Convention of the Protes-
tant Episcopal Church in the State of Delaware, held in Lewis-
Town, on Tuesday, the third day of May, 1796. Wilmington,
Printed by Peter Brynberg [1796]. § 7–13 p.; 8vo.

Copies: DeWE; DeWI (undated reprint); MCE.

415. Salzmann, Christian Gotthilf, 1744–1811.
    Elements of morality, for the use of children; with an intro-
ductory adress [!] to parents. Translated from the German of the
Rev. C. G. Salzmann [by Mary Wollstonecraft]. The third American edition. Wilmington, Printed by Joseph Johnson, Market-
Street, opposite the bank, 1796. § xiv, [15]–232 p.; 12mo.

Evans 31157.
Copies: DLC; DeHi; DeWI; MWA; PU.

416. Seven sages.
    Roman stories; or, The history of the seven wise masters of
Rome . . . The fiftieth edition. [Wilmington] Printed for, and sold

by James Wilson, bookbinder, etc., No. 5 High-Street, opposite the Upper-Market, 1796. § 103 p.; 12mo.

Bristol (Evans 47913).
Copies: DeHi.

417. A tribute to the memory of Doctor Joseph Capelle; taken from a paper printed at Wilmington, Delaware, of November 14, 1796. [Wilmington, 1796]. § Broadside.

Copies: DeHi.

418. The unfortunate concubines; or, The history of fair Rosamond . . . and Jane Shore . . . Wilmington, Printed and sold by Peter Brynberg, 1796. § 140 p.; 16mo.

Bristol (Evans 47944).
Copies: MWA.

419. WASHINGTON, GEORGE, PRES. U.S., 1732–1799.
Address of George Washington, President of the United States, and late Commander in Chief of the American army, to the people of the United States, preparatory to his declination. Wilmington, Printed for James Wilson's wholesale and retail bookstore, 1796. § 23 p.; 8vo.

Hawkins B:68.
Copies: DeWI.

420. WASHINGTON, GEORGE, PRES. U.S., 1732–1799.
An address to the people of the United States. From George Washington, President. New-Castle, Printed by Samuel & John Adams, 1796. § 21 p.; 4to.

Evans 31534.
Copies: DLC; DeGE; DeHi; DeWI; NN.

421. WATTS, ISAAC, 1674–1748.
Hymns and spiritual songs. In three books. I. Collected from the Scriptures. II. Composed on divine subjects. III. Prepared for the Lord's Supper. By I. Watts . . . Wilmington, Printed and sold by Peter Brynberg, 1796. § 242, [10] p.; 16mo.

Evans 48024.
Copies: DeWI; MWA.

422. WILLISON, JOHN, 1680–1750.
The afflicted man's companion; or, A directory for persons and families, afflicted with sickness or any other distress. With directions to the sick, both under and after affliction. Also, directions to the friends of the sick, and others who visit them. And likewise to all, how to prepare both for sickness and death . . . Wilmington, Printed by Joseph Johnson, 1796. § 272 p.; 12mo.

Evans 31641.
Copies: DeHi; DeU; DeWI; MWA; PHi; RPJCB.

423. WILMINGTON, DEL. RELIANCE FIRE COMPANY.
Articles for the Reliance Fire Company. Wilmington, Bonsal & Niles, printers, Market-Street [1796]. § Broadside; 41 by 33 cm.

Dated: 18th March, 1796.

Copies: DeHi.

424. WOLLSTONECRAFT, MARY, 1759–1797.
Letters written during a short residence in Sweden, Norway, and Denmark. By Mary Wollstonecraft. First American edition. Wilmington, Printed for & sold by J. Wilson, & J. Johnson, 1796. § 218, [6], 12 p.; 12mo.

Evans 31653.
Copies: DLC; De(M); DeGE; DeHi; DeU; DeWI; DeWin; KyLx; MWA; RPJCB.

1797

425. American academy of compliments; or, The complete American secretary. With a collection of the newest songs. Wilmington, Printed by Peter Brynberg, 1797.

Evans 31717.
No copy known.

426.　ARABIAN NIGHTS.

Arabian nights entertainments. Consisting of a collection of stories, told by the sultaness of the Indies, to divert the sultan from the execution of bloody vow he had made to marry a lady every day, and have her cut off next morning, to avenge himself for the disloyalty of his first sultaness. Containing a better account of the customs, manners, and religion of the eastern nations, viz. Tartars, Persians and Indians, than hitherto published. Translated into French from the Arabian mss. by Mr. Galland, of the Royal Academy; and now into English from the Paris edition. Wilmington, Printed and sold by Peter Brynberg, 1797. § 180 p.; 12mo.

Evans 31742.
Copies: DLC; DeWin.

427.　BIBLE.

The Holy Bible abridged; or, The history of the Old and New Testament. Illustrated with notes, and adorned with cuts for the use of children. Wilmington, Printed and sold by Peter Brynberg, 1797. § 134, [2] p.; 24mo.

Evans 31809.
Copies: CtY; DeWI; MWA; PP.

428.　BIBLE. N.T.

New Testament of our Lord and Saviour Jesus Christ, translated out of the original Greek: and with the former translations diligently compared and revised. Appointed to be read in churches. Wilmington, Printed and sold by Peter Brynberg, 1797. § 336 p.; 24mo.

Bristol (Evans 48061).
Copies: DeWI; KU.

429.　BIBLE. O.T. PSALMS.

Psalms, carefully suited to the Christian worship in the United States of America. Being Dr. Watts' imitation of the Psalms of David, as improved by Mr. Barlow. To this edition are added the words of sundry anthems . . . Wilmington, Printed and sold by Peter Brynberg, 1797. § [2], 287, [20] p.; 24mo.

Bristol, p. 561; Evans 31812; Hawkins B:93.
Copies: DLC; DeWI; MWA.

430. BROOM, JACOB, 1752–1810.
By legislative authority: a lottery! For raising four thousand dollars, clear of all expenses for the purpose of aiding the subscriber in the re-establishment of his cotton manufactory . . . Wilmington, Delaware, July 24, 1797. [Wilmington? Printed by Samuel and John Adams? 1797]. § Broadside; 31 by 24 cm.

Evans 31875.
Copies: PHi.

431. The Columbian almanac; or, The North-American calendar, for the year of our Lord 1798 . . . Wilmington, Printed and sold by Peter Brynberg, in Market-Street [1797]. § [36] p.; 12mo.

Evans 31956.
Copies: DLC; DeWI; DeWin; PPL.

432. DELAWARE. GENERAL ASSEMBLY. HOUSE.
Journal of the House of Representatives of the State of Delaware, at a session of the General Assembly, which was begun and held at Dover, on Tuesday, the third day of January, and ended on Tuesday, the twenty-fourth day of the same month, in the year of our Lord one thousand seven hundred and ninety-seven . . . New-Castle, Printed by Samuel and John Adams, 1797. § 57, 13, 22–27 p.; 8 fold. tables; 4to.

Contains George Washington's *To the people of United States* (Sept. 17, 1796) 13 p., and *Auditor's report*, 1796, p. 22–27.

Evans 32028.
Copies: De; DeHi; DeWI.

433. DELAWARE. GENERAL ASSEMBLY. HOUSE.
Journal of the House of Representatives of the State of Delaware, at a session of the General Assembly, which was begun and held at Dover, on Wednesday, the thirty-first day of May, and ended on Saturday, the third day of June, in the year of our Lord

one thousand seven hundred and ninety-seven . . . New-Castle, Printed by Samuel and John Adams, 1797. § 12 p.; 4to.

Hawkins B:74 (included in Evans 32028).
Copies: De; DeHi; DeWI (imperfect).

434.   DELAWARE. GENERAL ASSEMBLY. SENATE.
    Journal of the Senate of the State of Delaware, at a session of the General Assembly, commenced and held at Dover, on Wednesday, the ninth day of November, in the year of our Lord one thousand seven hundred and ninety-six . . . New-Castle, Printed by Samuel and John Adams, 1797. § 10 p.; 4to.

Evans 32029; Hawkins B:75.
Copies: DLC; De; DeHi.

435.   DELAWARE. GENERAL ASSEMBLY. SENATE.
    Journal of the Senate of the State of Delaware, at a session of the General Assembly, commenced and held at Dover, on Tuesday, the third day of January, in the year of our Lord one thousand seven hundred and ninety-seven. [New Castle, Printed by Samuel and John Adams, 1797]. § [13]–49 p.; 4to.

Paged in continuation of *Senate Journal* of Nov., 1796.

Hasse, p. 6.
Copies: DLC; De; DeHi.

436.   DELAWARE. LAWS.
    An act for establishing the boundaries of the town of New-Castle, and for other purposes therein mentioned. Also, an additional supplement to the act, intitled, "An act for the better regulation of the roads in the county of Kent." New-Castle, Printed by Samuel and John Adams [1797]. § 12 p.; 4to.

"Passed June 3, 1797."

Copies: DLC.

437.   DELAWARE. LAWS.
    Laws of the State of Delaware, passed at a session of the General Assembly, which was begun and held at Dover, on Tuesday, the third day of January, and ended on Tuesday, the twenty-

fourth day of the same month, in the year of our Lord one thousand seven hundred and ninety-seven . . . New-Castle, Printed by Samuel & John Adams, 1797. § 57 p.; 4to.

Evans 32031.
Copies: DLC; NNB.

438.   DELAWARE. LAWS.
Laws of the State of Delaware, from the fourteenth day of October, one thousand seven hundred, to the eighteenth day of August, one thousand seven hundred and ninety-seven. In two volumes . . . New-Castle, Printed by Samuel and John Adams, 1797. § 2 v.; 4to.

Evans 32030.
Copies: DLC; De; DeGE; DeHi; DeWI; MWA; NN; PPAmP; PPT.

439.   The Delaware and Eastern-Shore advertiser. No. 276, Monday, January 2 [–no. 379, Thursday, December 28, 1797]. Wilmington, Printed by Samuel & John Adams, corner of King and High-Streets, 1797. § fol.; semi-weekly.

Evans 32032.
Copies: DeHi; DeU (microfilm); DeWI.

440.   The Delaware gazette. No. 693, Wednesday, January 4 [–no. 792, Saturday, December 30, 1797]. Wilmington, Printed by W. C. Smyth, two doors below Mr. Brinton's tavern, High-Street, 1797. § fol.; semi-weekly.

Evans 32033.
Copies: DLC; DeHi; MH.

441.   DELAWARE GAZETTE.
The news-boy's address to the subscribers. Wilmington, Delaware gazette-office, 1797. § Broadside; 44 by 18 cm.

Dated: January 4, 1797.

Copies: DeHi.

THE

LETTERS

OF

FABIUS,

IN 1788,

ON THE FEDERAL CONSTITUTION;

AND

IN 1797,

ON THE PRESENT SITUATION

OF

PUBLIC AFFAIRS.
BY JOHN DICKINSON

Copy-Right Secured.

FROM THE OFFICE OF THE DELAWARE
GAZETTE, WILMINGTON,
BY W. C. SMYTH.

1797.

442.   [DICKINSON, JOHN] 1732–1808.
    The letters of Fabius, in 1788, on the federal Constitution; and in 1797, on the present situation of public affairs . . . Wilmington, From the office of the Delaware gazette, by W. C. Smyth, 1797. § iv, 202, [1] p.; 8vo.

Also a copy at DeWI with John Dickinson's name printed on the title page below the words "public affairs."

Evans 32042.
Copies: CSmH; DLC; DeGE; DeU; DeWI; MWA; NN; PHi; PPL; RPJCB.

443.   DILWORTH, THOMAS, d. 1780.
    The schoolmaster's assistant: being a compendium of arithmetic, both practical and theoretical. In five parts . . . Wilmington, Printed and sold by Peter Brynberg [1797?]. § [6], 192, [1] p.; 12mo.

Copies: MWA.

444.   [DODSLEY, ROBERT] 1703–1764.
    The oeconomy of human life, complete in two parts . . . Translated from an Indian manuscript, written by an ancient Bramin. To which is prefixed, an account of the manner in which the said manuscript was discovered. In a letter from an English gentleman residing in China, to the Earl of *******. Wilmington, Printed and sold by Peter Brynberg, 1797. § 94 p.; 12mo.

Evans 32061.
Copies: DeHi; MWA.

445.   ELLWOOD, THOMAS, 1639–1713.
    Davideis; the life of David, King of Israel: a sacred poem. In five books . . . Wilmington, Printed by Johnson & Preston, No. 73, Market-Street, 1797. § vi, [7]–159 p.; 12mo.

Evans 32079.
Copies: DLC; De(M); DeHi; DeU; DeWI; MWA; NN; PHi; PPL; PU; RPJCB.

446. ERRA PATER.

The book of knowledge; treating of the wisdom of the ancients. In four parts. Written by Erra Pater, a Jew: doctor in astronomy and physic; born in Bethany, near Mount Olivet in Judea. Made English by W. Lilly, student in physic and astrology. Wilmington, Printed and sold by Peter Brynberg, 1797. § 132 p.; 12mo.

Evans 32090.
Copies: DeWI.

447. The federal primer. Wilmington, Printed by Peter Brynberg, 1797.

Evans 32120.
No copy known.

448. FISHER, GEORGE, fl. 1731.

The instructor; or, Young man's best companion. Containing spelling, reading, writing and arithmetic . . . also merchants accompts . . . Likewise the practical gauger . . . to which are added, the family's best companion; and a compendium of geography and astronomy; also some useful interest tables. By George Fisher, accomptant. Wilmington, Printed and sold by Peter Brynberg, 1797. § xi, 360 p.; 12mo.

Evans 32840 (erroneously ascribed to Mrs. Ann (Fisher) Slack).
Copies: DeHi; DeWI; MWA; NNC; RPJCB.

449. Funny stories; or, The American jester, being a companion for a merry good fellow. Containing choice stories, funny anecdotes, wise sayings, & smart repartees . . . Wilmington, Printed for booksellers, country storekeepers, &c. &c. [by Peter Brynberg, 1797?]. § 144 p.; 12mo.

Running title: The funny companion.

Evans 32166.
Copies: DeWI.

450. GESSNER, SALOMON, 1730–1788.

The death of Abel. In five books. Attempted from the German of Mr. Gessner, by Mary Collyer. Wilmington, Printed and sold by Peter Brynberg, 1797. § 108 p.; 12mo.

Evans 32188.
Copies: DeWI; PU.

451. HELLENBROEK, ABRAHAM, 1658–1731.

Specimen of divine truths, fitted for the use of those, of various capacities, who desire to prepare themselves for a due confession of their faith . . . Translated from the Dutch . . . Wilmington, Printed by Peter Brynberg, 1797.

Evans 32244.
No copy known.

452. HERVEY, JAMES, 1714–1758.

The beauties of Hervey; or, Descriptive, picturesque and instructive passages, selected from the works of this deservedly admired author . . . To which are added, Memoirs of the author's life and character; with an elegiac poem on his death . . . Wilmington, Printed by Peter Brynberg, 1797. § xi, [12]–226, [2], [4] p.; 12mo.

Evans 32249.
Copies: DeHi; DeWI; DeWin; MWA; MiU-C; NN; PCC; PHi; PPL; PV; RPJCB.

453. HERVEY, JAMES, 1714–1758.

Meditations and contemplations. In two volumes. Containing, volume I. Meditations among the tombs. Reflections on a flower garden; and, A descant upon creation. Volume II. Contemplations on the night. Contemplations on the starry-heavens; and, A winter piece . . . Wilmington, Printed and sold by Peter Brynberg, 1797. § 2 v. in 1 (428 p.); 12mo.

Evans 32250.
Copies: DLC; DeHi; DeU; DeWI; DeWin; MWA; NN; RPJCB.

454. The history of Jane Shore, and fair Rosamond. Wilmington, Printed by Peter Brynberg, 1797.

Evans 32255.
No copy known.

455. [HOWARD, THOMAS].
The history of the seven wise mistresses of Rome. Containing many ingenious and entertaining stories; wherein the treachery of evil counsellors is discovered, innocency cleared, and the wisdom of the seven wise mistresses displayed. Wilmington, Printed and sold by Peter Brynberg, 1797.

Evans 32286.
No copy known.

456. KEACH, BENJAMIN, 1640–1704.
The travels of true godliness, from the beginning of the world, to this present day. In an apt and pleasant allegory. Shewing what true godliness is; also, the troubles, oppositions, reproaches, and persecution he hath met with in every age. Together with the danger and sad declining state he is in at this present time, by errors, heresies, and ungodliness, or open profaneness . . . Wilmington, Printed by Peter Brynberg, for John Boggs, Minister of the Gospel, 1797. § iv, 5–234 p.; 12mo.

Evans 32327.
Copies: DeHi; DeWI; MWA; NN; PU.

457. LAWS, JOHN.
An inaugural dissertation on the rationale of the operation of opium on the animal economy; with observations on its use in disease. Submitted to the examination of . . . the trustees and medical faculty of the University of Pennsylvania. Wilmington, Printed by W. C. Smyth, 1797. § 12 p.; 8vo.

Evans 32364.
Copies: DLC; DNLM; MH; PPAmP; PPC.

458. MARTINET, JOHANNES FLORENTIUS, 1729–1795.
The catechism of nature; for the use of children. By Doctor Martinet, professor of philosophy at Zutphen. Translated from the

Dutch . . . Wilmington, Printed and sold by Peter Brynberg, 1797. § 72 p.; 12mo.

Evans 32428.
Copies: DeU; DeWI; MWA.

459. MOORE, JOHN HAMILTON, d. 1807.
   The young gentleman and lady's monitor, and English teacher's assistant: being a collection of select pieces from our best modern writers . . . Particularly adapted for the use of our eminent schools and accademies [!] as well as private persons . . . The latest edition. By J. Hamilton Moore . . . Wilmington, Printed and sold by Peter Brynberg, 1797. § vi, [7]–392, [4] p.; 4 plates; 12mo.

Evans 32495.
Copies: DLC; DeHi; MWA; PHi (now in PPL).

460. NEW CASTLE CO., DEL.
   List of rates for innkeepers in the County of New-Castle, as settled by the justices of the Court of General Sessions of the Peace, at New-Castle, in the May sessions, one thousand seven hundred and ninety seven . . . New-Castle, S. & J. Adams, printers [1797]. § Broadside; 14 cm.

Bristol (Evans 48204).
Copies: DeHi.

461. The New-England primer; or, An easy and pleasant guide to the art of reading. Wilmington, Printed by Peter Brynberg, 1797.

Evans 32531.
No copy known.

462. PROTESTANT EPISCOPAL CHURCH IN THE U.S.A. DELAWARE (DIOCESE).
Journal of the proceedings of the Seventh Convention of the Protestant Episcopal Church in the State of Delaware, held at Middle-Town, on Tuesday, the second of May, 1797. Wilmington, Printed by Peter Brynberg [1797]. § 15–20 p.; 8vo.

Copies: DeWE; DeWI (undated reprint); MCE.

463. RUSSELL, ROBERT, OF WADHURST, SUSSEX.

Seven sermons, viz. I. Of the unpardonable sin against the Holy Ghost . . . II. The saint's duty and exercise . . . III. The accepted time and day of salvation. IV. The end of time, and beginning of eternity. V. Joshua's resolution to serve the Lord. VI. The way to heaven made plain. VII. The future state of man . . . By Robert Russel [!] . . . Wilmington, Printed by Peter Brynberg, 1797. § 18mo.

Evans 32788.
No copy known.

464. SCOTT, JOB, 1751–1793.

Journal of the life, travels and gospel labours of that faithful servant and minister of Christ, Job Scott. Wilmington, Printed and sold by Bonsal & Niles, 1797. § x, [2], 324 p.; 12mo.

Evans 32811.
Copies: DeHi; DeU; DeWF; DeWI; MWA; PHC; PPL; PSC-Hi.

465. SCOTT, WILLIAM, 1750–1804.

Lessons in elocution; or, A selection of pieces, in prose and verse, for the improvement of youth in reading and speaking. By William Scott. The seventh American edition. To which are prefixed, Elements of gesture. Illustrated by four elegant copperplates; and rules for expressing, with propriety, the various passions and emotions of the mind. [By John Walker]. Wilmington, Printed and sold by Peter Brynberg, 1797. § viii, [9]–383 p.; 4 plates; 12mo.

Evans 32814.
Copies: CSmH; DLC; DeWI; MWA.

466. SEVEN SAGES.

History of the seven wise masters of Rome, containing many ingenious and entertaining stories, wherein the treachery of evil counsellors is discovered, innocency cleared, and the wisdom of the seven wise masters displayed. Wilmington, Printed by Peter Brynberg, 1797.

Evans 32803.
No copy known.

467. SIBBES, RICHARD, 1577–1635.
Divine meditations and holy contemplations: by R. Sibbes,
D.D., on the Philadelphia plague. On the day of judgement . . . Wilmington, Printed by Bonsal & Niles, for Molleston Correy, 1797.
§ 60 p.; 12mo.

Bristol (Evans 48253).
Copies: PPL.

468. SOCIETY FOR THE SUPPRESSION OF VICE AND IMMO-
RALITY.
Constitution of the Society for the Suppression of Vice and
Immorality . . . [Wilmington, 1797]. § Broadside; 42 by 33 cm.

Dated by the Historical Society of Delaware: March 18, 1797.

Copies: DeHi.

469. The syren, or Vocal enchantress: being a collection of the
newest and most admired miscellaneous, – pathetic, and
passionate, – anacreontic and jovial, – comic, ingenious, and witty,
– sea, hunting, and Masonic songs. Selected from the most approved . . . publications; including the best songs of Dibdin Edwin,
&c. Wilmington, Printed for and sold by James Wilson, bookseller and stationer, No. 5, High-Street, opposite the Upper Market House, 1797. § 38, 36, 24, 48, 28, [6] p.; 12mo.

"Printed for Bonsal & Niles and James Wilson": on added title
pages for parts I–V.

Evans 32901.
Copies: DeWI; MWA.

470. The syren, or Vocal enchantress: being a collection of the
newest and most admired miscellaneous, – pathetic, and
passionate, – anacreontic and jovial, – comic, ingenious, and witty,
– sea, hunting, and Masonic songs. Selected from the most approved sentimental, humorous, and ingenious publications; including all the best songs of Dibdin Edwin, &c. Wilmington, Printed
by Bonsal and Niles, in Market-Street, 1797. § 3 p. l., 38, 36, 24,
48, 28, [6] p.; 12mo.

Copies: MH.

471. TAPLIN, WILLIAM, d. 1807.
      A compendium of practical and experimental farriery, orig-
inally suggested by reason and confirmed by practice. Equally
adapted for the convenience of the gentleman, the farmer, the
groom and the smith . . . Wilmington, Printed by Bonsal & Niles,
for Robert Campbell, bookseller, Philadelphia, 1797. § viii, 290,
[6], [12] p.; fold. front.; 12mo.

Evans 32906.
Copies: CSmH; DLC; DeU; DeWI; DeWin; MWA; NN; PU;
RPJCB.

472. TOM THUMB.
      The history of Thomas Thumb, with his wonderful adven-
tures; and some anecdotes respecting Grumbo, the great giant.
Wilmington, Printed by James Adams, north side of the Upper
Market House, 1797. § 30 p.; illus.; 32mo.

Evans 32931.
Copies: PHi (now in PPL); PPL; PU.

473. The United States' almanac, or The North-American calen-
      dar; for the year of our Lord 1798 . . . Wilmington, Printed
and sold wholesale, by James Adams, north side of the Upper Market [1797]. § [36] p.; 12mo.

Evans 33101.
Copies: DLC; DeHi; DeWI; MWA.

474. The universal dream-book. Wilmington, Printed by Peter
      Brynberg, 1797.

Evans 33103.
No copy known.

475. Universal spelling-book. Wilmington, Printed by Peter
      Brynberg, 1797.

Evans 33105.
No copy known.

476. VALENTINE AND ORSON.
The history of Valentine and Orson, the two sons of the Emperor of Greece. Wilmington, Printed by Peter Brynberg, 1797.

Evans 33110.
No copy known.

477. VAUGHAN, JOHN, 1775–1807.
Observations on animal electricity. In explanation of the metallic operation of Doctor Perkins . . . Wilmington, From the office of the Delaware gazette, by W. C. Smyth, 1797. § 32 p.; 8vo.

Evans 33112.
Copies: DNLM; DeGE; MWA; NBM; NN.

478. WOOLMAN, JOHN, 1720–1772.
A first book for children, A.B.C.D. &c . . . Wilmington, Printed by Peter Brynberg, 1797.

Evans 33248.
No copy known.

479. ZIMMERMANN, JOHANN GEORG, RITTER VON, 1728–1795.
Solitude considered with respect to its influence upon the mind and the heart. Written originally in German by M. Zimmermann, aulic counsellor and physician to His Britannic Majesty at Hanover. Translated from the French of J. B. Mercier . . . Wilmington, Printed by Johnson & Preston, No. 73, Market-Street, 1797. § [4], v, 298 p.; 12mo.

Evans 33261.
Copies: CSmH; CtY; DLC; DeGE; DeHi; DeU; DeWI; DeWin; MWA; NN; PPL; RPJCB.

1798

480. BIBLE. N.T.
The New Testament of our Lord and Saviour Jesus Christ, translated out of the original Greek; and with the former transla-

tions diligently compared and revised . . . Wilmington, Printed and sold by Peter Brynberg, 1798. § 291, [1] p.; 12mo.

Evans 33416.
Copies: DeWI; DeWin; NN.

481. The Columbian almanac; or, The North American calendar for the year of our Lord 1799 . . . Wilmington, Printed and sold by Peter Brynberg, in Market-Street [1798]. § [48] p.; 12mo.

Evans 33539.
Copies: DLC; DeGE; DeHi; DeWI; MWA; PHi.

482. DELAWARE. GENERAL ASSEMBLY. HOUSE.
Journal of the House of Representatives of the State of Delaware, at a session of the General Assembly, which was begun and held at Dover, on Tuesday, the second day of January, and ended on Saturday, the twenty-seventh day of the same month, in the year of our Lord one thousand seven hundred and ninety-eight . . . New-Castle, Printed by Samuel and John Adams, 1798. § 71 p.; 14 fold. tables; fol.

Evans 33619.
Copies: DLC; De; NN.

483. DELAWARE. GENERAL ASSEMBLY. SENATE.
Journal of the Senate of the State of Delaware, at a session of the General Assembly, commenced and holden at Dover, on Tuesday, the second day of January, in the year of our Lord one thousand seven hundred and ninety-eight . . . New-Castle, Printed by Samuel and John Adams, 1798. § 49 p.; fol.

Evans 33620.
Copies: DLC; De; DeWI; MWA.

484. DELAWARE. LAWS.
Laws of the State of Delaware, passed at a session of the General Assembly, which was begun and held at Dover, on Tuesday the second day of January, and ended on Saturday the twenty-seventh day of the same month, in the year of our Lord one thou-

sand seven hundred and ninety-eight . . . New-Castle, Printed by Samuel and John Adams, 1798. § 43 p.; 4to.

Evans 33621.
Copies: CSmH; NHi; NNB; PPAmP.

485.   DELAWARE. LAWS.
    The militia law. New-Castle, Printed by Samuel and John Adams, 1798.

Evans 33622.
No copy known.

486.   The Delaware and Eastern-Shore advertiser. No. 380, Monday, January 1 [–no. 484, Monday, December 31, 1798].
Wilmington, Printed by Samuel and John Adams, corner of King and High-Streets, 1798. § fol.; semi-weekly.

Evans 33623.
Copies: DeHi; DeU (microfilm); DeWI.

487.   The Delaware gazette. No. 793, Wednesday, January 3 [–no. 894, Saturday, December 29, 1798]. Wilmington, Printed by W. C. Smyth, two doors below Mr. Brinton's tavern, High-Street, 1798. § fol.; semi-weekly.

Evans 33624.
Copies: DeHi; PPL.

488.   DILWORTH, THOMAS, d. 1780.
    The schoolmaster's assistant . . . with many additions . . . by James Gibbons. Wilmington, Peter Brynberg, 1798. § xvi, 228 p.; plate; 12mo.

Bristol (Evans 48413a).
Copies: DAU; DLC; MiU-C.

489.   DILWORTH, THOMAS, d. 1780.
    The young book-keeper's assistant: shewing him in the most plain and easy manner, the Italian way of stating debtor and creditor . . . The thirteenth edition . . . Wilmington, Printed by Peter Brynberg, 1798. § 1 v. (various pagings); 8vo.

Evans 33640.
Copies: DeHi; DeU; DeWI; MWA; PAtM; PHi; RPJCB.

490. GOUGH, JOHN, 1721–1791.
Practical arithmetick. In four books. I. Whole numbers, weights and measures. II. Fractions, vulgar and decimal. III. Mercantile arithmetick. IV. Extractions of roots, progressions, &c . . . Carefully revised by Thomas Telfair . . . And now fitted to the commerce of America. With an appendix of algebra, by the late W. Atdinson [!] . . . Dublin, Printed; Wilmington, Reprinted, and sold by Peter Brynberg, 1798. § iv, [5]–359 p.; 12mo.

Evans 33810.
Copies: CSmH; DLC.

491. HEMPHILL, WILLIAM, 1743–1823.
William Hemphill, of the Borough of Wilmington, having declined business, and in order to close all his accounts as soon as possible, requests all persons having any demands against him . . . to present the same within three months for settlement . . . At the same time he begs leave to recommend his son James . . . who has succeeded him in the grocery business . . . Wilmington, Printed by S. & J. Adams, 1798. § Broadside; 42 by 27 cm.

Dated: Wilmington, May 16, 1798.

Copies: DeHi; DeWI.

492. MAXWELL, ELIZABETH.
Notice. The subscribers, by public notice bearing date the seventh of June last, called on all persons having demands against the estate of Solomon Maxwell, esq., deceased, to bring in their accounts . . . New Castle, Samuel and John Adams, printers, 1798. § Broadside; 26 by 20 cm.

Dated: Christiana Bridge, Aug. 2, 1798; signed: Elizabeth Maxwell, Admx., James Couper, David Nivin, Robert Eakin, Admrs.

Copy: DeHi.

493. Plan of Wilmington and its environs. [Wilmington? 1798?]. 68 by 49 cm.

Scale ca. 1:6500.

The map was supposedly drawn by Joseph Warner and Samuel Nichols. The only copy known is a re-strike from the original plate in the Wilmington Institute Free Library, cf. *Every evening*, August 3, 1918, p. 3.

Copies: DeWI.

494. UNITED STATES.
    Role d'equipage, laid down agreeably to the decree of the Executive Directory of France. Wilmington, Printed by W. C. Smyth, 1798.

Evans 34845.
No copy known.

495. The United States almanac, or The North-American calendar, for the year of our Lord 1799 . . . Wilmington, Printed and sold wholesale by James Adams, north-side of the Upper Market [1798].

Copies: DeHi (imperfect).

496. Wilmington mercury. Printed occasionally and delivered gratis – to the patrons of the Delaware gazette. By Smyth . . . Wilmington, Printed by W. C. Smyth, 1798.

Evans 35036.
Copies: DeHi (18 issues, Sept. 18–Oct. 25, 1798); DeWin (Sept. 16, 29, 1798); NN (Sept. 23, 1798).

1799
═══════

497. The Columbian almanac; or, The North-American calendar, for the year of our Lord 1800 . . . Wilmington, Printed and sold by Peter Brynberg, in Market-Street [1799]. § 48 p.; 12mo.

Evans 35321.
Copies: DLC; DeHi; DeWI; DeWin; MdHi; PHi.

498.   Conversation cards; or, Ladies' & gentlemen's leisure hour's amusement. Wilmington, Printed by James Wilson, 1799.

Evans 35351.
No copy known.

499.   COSGRAVE, J.
A genuine history of the lives and actions of the most notorious Irish highwaymen, tories and rapparees, from Redmond O'Hanlon, the famous gentleman-robber, to Cahier na Gappul, the great horse-catcher . . . To which is added, The gold-finder; or, The history of Manus Mac Oneil . . . Wilmington, Printed and sold by Bonsal & Niles, 1799. § 140 p.; 24mo.

Evans 35355.
Copies: MWA.

500.   DELAWARE. GENERAL ASSEMBLY. HOUSE.
Journal of the House of Representatives of the State of Delaware, at a session of the General Assembly, which was begun and held at Dover, on Tuesday, the first day of January, and ended Saturday, the second day of February, in the year of our Lord one thousand seven hundred and ninety-nine . . . New-Castle, Printed by Samuel and John Adams, nearly opposite the Court-House, 1799. § 112, 66 p.; fol.

Report of finances of the State of Delaware: 66 p. at end.

Evans 35394.
Copies: DLC; De; NN.

501.   DELAWARE. GENERAL ASSEMBLY. SENATE.
Journal of the Senate of the State of Delaware, at a session of the General Assembly, commenced and holden at Dover, on Tuesday, the first day of January in the year of our Lord one thousand seven hundred and ninety-nine . . . New-Castle, Printed by S. and Jno. Adams, nearly opposite the Court-House, 1799. § 85 [i.e. 93] p.; fol.

Evans 35395.
Copies: DLC; De; DeWI; MWA; NN.

502. DELAWARE. LAWS.

The laws of the State of Delaware, from the earliest times to the year 1798; with an appendix, containing various public records, and certain legislative acts, which from their connection in some respects with the existing laws, require to be preserved. To which are prefixed, the Constitution of the United States, and the Constitution of the State of Delaware. New-Castle, Printed by Samuel and John Adams, 1799.

Evans 35396.
No copy known.

503. DELAWARE. LAWS.

Laws of the State of Delaware, passed at a session of the General Assembly, which was begun and held at Dover, on Tuesday, the first day of January, and ended Saturday the second day of February, in the year of our Lord one thousand seven hundred and ninety-nine . . . New-Castle, Printed by Samuel and John Adams, 1799. § [45]–113 p.; 4to.

Bristol (Evans 48834); Hawkins B:105.
Copies: CSmH; NNB; PPAmP; RPJCB.

504. The Delaware and Eastern-Shore advertiser. No. 485, Thursday, January 3 [–no. 578, December 26, 1799]. Wilmington, Printed by Samuel and John Adams, corner of King and High Streets, 1799. § fol.; semi-weekly.

Last issue located: No. 578, December 26, 1799.

Brigham, v. 1, p. 79–80; Evans 35397.
Copies: DeHi; DeU (microfilm); DeWI; MH; MWA.

505. The Delaware gazette. No. 895, Wednesday, March 14 [–no. 946, Saturday, September 7, 1799]. Wilmington, Printed by Bonsal & Niles for Vaughan & Coleman, Market-Street, 1799. § fol.; semi-weekly.

Evans 35398.
Copies: DLC; DeHi; NHi.

506. DILWORTH, THOMAS, d. 1780.
A new guide to the English tongue: in five parts . . . Wilmington, Printed and sold by Peter Brynberg, 1799. § v, [6]–142 p.; front. (port.), illus.; 12mo.

Evans 35409.
Copies: DLC.

507. DILWORTH, THOMAS, d. 1780.
The schoolmasters assistant: being a compendium of arithmetic, both practical and theoretical. In five parts . . . Wilmington, Printed and sold by Bonsal and Niles. Also sold at their book-store, No. 173, Market-Street, Baltimore [1799]. § [6], 192 p.; port., fold. table; 12mo.

Evans 35411.
Copies: DLC; DeGE; DeWI; MH; MWA; MiU-C; PHi (now in PPL); PU; RPJCB.

508. FENNING, DANIEL.
The ready reckoner or, Trader's useful assistant, in buying and selling all sorts of commodities. Either wholesale or retail. Shewing at one view, the amount or value of any number or quantity of goods or merchandise, from one up to ten thousand, at the various prices, from a farthing to 20 s. either by the hundred, half hundred or quarter, pound or ounce, ell or yard, &c., &c . . . 12th ed. Wilmington, Printed and sold by Peter Brynberg, 1799. § 189, [3] p.; 12mo.

Evans 35477.
Copies: De(M); DeU; DeWI; MWA; PHi.

509. FRANKLIN, BENJAMIN, 1706–1790.
The life of Doctor Benjamin Franklin. Written by himself. Fourth American edition. Wilmington, Printed and sold by Peter Brynberg, 1799. § iv, [5]–178, [1] p.; 12mo.

Evans 35497.
Copies: DLC; DeWI; PHi (now in PPL); PPAmP.

510. Friend of the people. Vol. 1, no. 1, September 14 [– 1799]. Dover, William Black, 1799. § Semi-weekly.

Only issue located is vol. 1, no. 5, September 28, 1799, cf. Brigham, v. 1, p. 78.

Copies: MH.

511. JESS, ZACHARIAH.
The American tutor's assistant, improved; or, A compendious system of decimal, practical arithmetic; comprising the usual methods of calculation, with the addition of federal money, and other decimals . . . Wilmington, Printed and sold by Bonsal and Niles. Also sold at their book-store, No. 173, Market Street, Baltimore, 1799. § [4], 204 p.; 12mo.

Evans 35669.
Copies: DLC; DeWI; MWA.

512. JESS, ZACHARIAH.
A compendious system of practical surveying, and dividing of land: concisely defined, methodically arranged, and fully exemplified. The whole adapted for the easy and regular instruction of youth, in our American schools . . . Wilmington, Printed by Bonsal and Niles for the compiler, 1799. § v, [3], 12 [i.e. 212] p.; 8vo.

Evans 35670.
Copies: DLC; DeGE; DeHi; DeU; DeWI; DeWin; MWA; NN; NjP; PPF; PPL; PU.

513. Mirror of the times, & general advertiser. Vol. 1, no. 1, Wednesday, November 20 [–no. 12, Saturday, December 28, 1799]. Wilmington, Printed by James Wilson, south side of the Upper Market, High-Street, 1799. § fol.; semi-weekly.

Evans 35827.
Copies: DeGE (microfilm); DeHi; NN.

514. [ROBERTSON, JOHN] 1712–1796.
Tables of difference of latitude and departure: constructed to every quarter of a degree of the quadrant, and continued from one, to the distance of one hundred miles or chains. Wilmington, Printed by Bonsal and Niles, for Zachariah Jess, 1799. § [1], 91, [3], 60 p.; 8vo.

Usually bound with Jess, *A compendious system of practical surveying*.
Evans 36236.
Copies: DLC; DeGE; DeHi; MWA; NN; NjP; PPF; PPL; PU; RPJCB.

515. RUTH, WILLIAM.
    Twenty-five dollars reward. Made their escape from the gaol of New-Castle County on Sunday the 18th inst. two Negro men and a white boy . . . New-Castle, Printed by S. & Jno. Adams, nearly opposite the Court-House [1799]. § Broadside; 35 by 25 cm.
Signed: William Ruth, Gaoler. New-Castle, Aug. 19, 1799.

Bristol (Evans 48959).
Copies: PPL.

516. The town and country almanac for the year of our Lord 1800 . . . Wilmington, Printed and sold by Bonsal & Niles [1799]. § [48] p.; 12mo.

Evans 36442.
Copies: CtY; DLC; DeHi; MWA.

517. [VAUGHAN, JOHN] 1775–1807.
    Chemical syllabus. [Wilmington, Bonsal & Niles, printers, 1799]. § 21 p.; 12mo.

Dedication dated: November 20, 1799.

Evans 36609.
Copies: DLC; DeGE; DeHi; DeWI; MBAt; MiU-C; NN; PPAmP; PPL; PU.

1800

518. Address to the citizens of Kent, on the approaching election. [Wilmington, Printed at the Franklin Press, by James Wilson, 1800]. § 14 p.; 8vo.

Peregrine Letherbury, chairman of the committee of the Democratic Party of Kent County appointed to prepare the address.

182   [1800]

Evans 36768.
Copies: DLC; MBAt.

519. The American jest book: containing a choice selection of jests, anecdotes, bon mots, stories, advertisements, songs, epigrams &c . . . A new edition, enlarged and improved. Wilmington, Printed and sold by Bonsal & Niles – also sold at their bookstore, No. 173, Market-Street, Baltimore, 1800. § 120 p.; 12mo.

Evans 36815.
Copies: DLC; MWA.

520. ARABIAN NIGHTS.
Arabian nights entertainments . . . Translated into French from Arabian MSS. by Mr. Galland . . . and now into English from the Paris edition. Wilmington, Printed and sold by Bonsal & Niles – also sold at their book-store, No. 173, Market-Street, Baltimore, 1800. § 156 p.; 12mo.

Bristol (Evans 49006); N.Y. Pub. Libr. 1277.
Copies: NN.

521. AULNOY, MARIE CATHERINE (JUMELLE DE BERNE- VILLE) COMTESSE D', 1650?–1705.
The history of the tales of the fairies. Newly done from the French. Wilmington, Printed by P. Brynberg, 1800. § 141 p.; 12mo.

Evans 36863.
Copies: DeWI.

522. BARBAULD, ANNA LETITIA (AIKIN) 1743–1825.
Evening tales, consisting of miscellaneous pieces for the amusement and instruction of children, extracted from the works of Mrs. Barbauld and Mr. Aikin. Wilmington, Printed and sold by Peter Brynberg [1800?]. § 106, 1 p.; 16mo.

Bristol (Evans 49015).
Copies: MWA; PP.

523. [BARBAULD, ANNA LETITIA (AIKIN)] 1743–1825.
Lessons for children, part II. From four to five years old. Wilmington, Printed and sold wholesale and retail by James Wil-

son, at the Mirror book-store and printing-office, 1800. § 44 p.;
illus.; 24mo.

Evans 36890.
Copies: MWA.

524. [BECKLEY, JOHN JAMES] 1757–1807.
An epitome of the life & character of Thomas Jefferson.
[Wilmington, Printed by James Wilson, at the Franklin Press,
1800] § 8 p.; 4to.

Signed: Americanus. Pennsylvania, July, 1800.

Evans 36921.
Copies: DLC; DeHi; PPL.

525. BEDFORD, GUNNING, 1747–1812.
A funeral oration upon the death of General Washington,
prepared at the request of the Masonic Lodge, no. 14, of Wilmington . . . and delivered . . . the 27th of December, anno lucis 5799;
and now published at the particular desire of the Lodge. Wilmington, Printed at the Franklin Press, by James Wilson, 1800. § 19 p.;
4to.

Evans 36922.
Copies: MBFM.

526. [BERINGTON, SIMON] 1680–1755.
The adventures of Signor Gaudentio di Lucca. Being the
substance of his examination before the fathers of the Inquisition,
at Bologna, in Italy. Giving an account of an unknown country in
the midst of the desarts [!] of Africa. Copied from the original
manuscript in St. Mark's library, at Venice. With critical notes by
the learned Signor Rhedi. Translated from the Italian. Wilmington, Printed and sold by Bonsal & Niles, 1800. § xxi, [23]–234 p.;
12mo.

Evans 36945.
Copies: CtY; DLC; DeU; DeWI; MWA; MdHi; NN; PPPD.

527. BIBLE. O.T. PSALMS.
The whole book of Psalms, in metre; with hymns suited to
the feasts and fasts of the church, and other occasions of public wor-

ship. Wilmington, Printed by Peter Brynberg [1800]. § [2], 226, [2] p.; 16mo.

Bound usually with: Protestant Episcopal Church in the U.S.A. *The book of common prayer* (no. 554).

Evans 38337.
Copies: CSmH; DLC; DeU; DeWI.

528. Bonsal and Niles' Town and country almanac, for the year of our Lord, 1801 . . . Wilmington, Printed and sold by Bonsal and Niles, Market-Street [1800]. § [48] p.; 12mo.

Drake 1409.
Copies: DeHi; PHi (now in PPL).

529. BRINGHURST, JOSEPH.
For sale, in Wilmington, on the west side of Market-Street, two doors below the Upper Market-House, by Joseph Bringhurst, Jun., loaf and Muscovado sugars, molasses, wines of the first quality . . . Wilmington, Printed by Bonsal & Niles, Market-Street [1800?]. § Broadside; 12 by 8 cm.

Copies: De; DeGE; DeHi.

530. CAMPBELL, THOMAS, 1777–1844.
The pleasures of hope, with other poems . . . The third American edition. Wilmington, Printed at the Franklin Press, by James Wilson, 1800. § 56 p.; 12mo.

Evans 37092.
Copies: DLC; DeHi; DeU; DeWI; MWA; NHi.

531. The Columbian almanac; or, The North-American calendar, for the year of our Lord 1801 . . . Wilmington, Printed and sold by Peter Brynberg, Market-Street [1800]. § 48 p.; 12mo.

Evans 37206.
Copies: DLC; DeGE; DeWI; MH; MWA; MWiW; NHi; NN; PHi (now in PPL).

532.   . . . The Committee appointed to draft an address to the
citizens of the third election district of Chester County,
having taken the same into serious consideration, offer the following . . . ticket for your consideration and support . . . Wilmington,
Printed at the Franklin Press by James Wilson, 1800. § Broadside; 32 by 13 cm.

Imprint at head of title; dated: Chatham-Inn, London Grove
Township, September 23, 1800.

Evans 37218.
Copies: MWA.

533.   [DAVIDSON, JAMES] 1732–1809.
A short introduction to Latin grammar, for the use of the
University and Academy of Pennsylvania in Philadelphia . . . Sev-
enth edition, corrected and revised. Wilmington, Printed and sold
by Bonsal & Niles – also sold at their book-store, No. 173, Market-
Street, Baltimore, 1800. § 108 p.; 12mo.

Evans 38501.
Copies: CtY; MWA; MdBS; MdHi; RPJCB.

534.   DELAWARE. GENERAL ASSEMBLY. HOUSE.
Journal of the House of Representatives of the State of Delaware, at a session of the General Assembly, begun and holden at
Dover, on Tuesday, the seventh day of January and ended on Saturday the twenty-fifth day of the same month, in the year of our
Lord one thousand eight hundred . . . New-Castle, Printed by Samuel and John Adams, nearly opposite the Court-House, 1800. § 85,
114 p.; fol.

"A report of the finances of the State of Delaware, for the year
1799," 114 p. at end.

Evans 37310.
Copies: DLC; De; NN.

535.   DELAWARE. GENERAL ASSEMBLY. SENATE.
Journal of the Senate of the State of Delaware, at a session
of the General Assembly, commenced and holden at Dover, on
Tuesday the seventh day of January, in the year of our Lord one

thousand eight hundred . . . New-Castle, Printed by Samuel and John Adams, nearly opposite the Court-House, 1800. § 59 p.; fol.

Evans 37311.
Copies: DLC; De; DeWI; MWA; NN.

536.   DELAWARE. LAWS.

Laws of the State of Delaware, passed at a session of the General Assembly, which was begun and held at Dover, on Tuesday the seventh, and ended on Saturday the twenty-fifth day of January, in the year of our Lord one thousand eight hundred . . . Dover, Printed by W. Black, 1800. § 117–139 p.; 4to.

Evans 37312.
Copies: CSmH; DeHi; NNB.

537.   DILWORTH, THOMAS, d. 1780.

The schoolmasters assistant: being a compendium of arithmetic, both practical and theoretical. In five parts . . . Wilmington, Printed and sold by Peter Brynberg [1800?]. § [8], 192 p.; front. (port.), fold. tables; 12mo.

A list of books printed and sold is at the end, including Fisher's *Arithmetic*, which was published by Brynberg in 1800.

Hawkins B:123.
Copies: DeWI; NN.

538.   ENTICK, JOHN, 1703–1773.

Entick's new English spelling dictionary, teaching to write and pronounce the English tongue with ease and propriety . . . with a list of proper names of men and women . . . To which is prefixed a grammatical introduction to the English tongue. A new edition. Revised, corrected and enlarged. To which is added a catalogue of words of similar sounds, but of different spellings and significations. By William Crakelt . . . London, Printed; Wilmington, Reprinted and sold by Peter Brynberg, 1800. § xxx, 31–460 p.; 16mo.

Evans 37375.
Copies: DeWI; MWA; NN.

539. FISHER, GEORGE, fl. 1731.

Arithmetic, in the plainest and most concise methods hither-to extant: with new improvements for dispatch of business in all the several rules . . . London, Printed; Wilmington, Reprinted and sold by Peter Brynberg, Market-Street, 1800. § xii, 2, 11–312 p.; 12mo.

Evans 37424.
Copies: De(M); DeWI; MWA; MoHi.

540. FOTHERGILL, SAMUEL.

Discourses delivered extempore at several meeting houses of the people called Quakers. Wilmington, Printed by B. & J. John-son, No. 147 High-Street, 1800. § xv, [4], 270 p.; 12mo.

Copies: DeWI.

541. FRAZER, WILLIAM CLARK, d. 1838.

A funeral oration . . . in memory of . . . George Washington . . . delivered at Lancaster, on the 22nd of February last, to Lodge no. 43 . . . [Wilmington, Printed at the Franklin Press, by James Wilson, 1800]. § 15 p.; 8vo.

Evans 37448.
Copies: CSmH.

542. GOUGH, JOHN, 1721–1791.

Practical arithmetick in four books, I. Whole numbers, weights and measures. II. Fractions, vulgar and decimal. III. Mer-cantile arithmetick. IV. Extraction of roots, progression, &c . . . By John Gough . . . Carefully revised by Thomas Telfair . . . With an appendix of algebra, by the late W. Atkinson . . . Dublin, Printed; Wilmington, Re-printed and sold by Peter Brynberg, 1800. § iv, 5–359 p.; 12mo.

Evans 37535.
Copies: DeWI; MH; MWA; NcU; PP.

543. HARRISON, RALPH, 1748–1810.

Rudiments of English grammar, containing, I. The differ-ent kinds, relations and changes of words. II. Syntax, or the right construction of sentences: with an appendix, comprehending a table of verbs irregularly inflected . . . By Mr. Harrison. A new edition with additions and improvements by an eminent hand. Wilmington, Printed and sold by James Wilson [1800?]. § iv, [2], [7]–107, [1] p.; 18mo.

Assigned to [1800?] on the basis of printer's advertisement at end of volume, which lists a number of works known in editions of 1800. Previously dated as [1788?] by CSmH and DLC, and as [1796?] by Hawkins.

Bristol, p. 396, and 546; Hawkins B:63.
Copies: CSmH; DLC; DeWI.

544. JESS, ZACHARIAH.
The American tutor's assistant, improved; or, A compendious system of decimal, practical arithmetic; comprising the usual methods of calculation; with the addition of federal money, and other decimals . . . Second edition, corrected and revised by the compiler. Wilmington, Printed and sold by Bonsal and Niles. Also sold at their book-store, No. 173, Market-Street, Baltimore, 1800. [4], 204 p.; 12mo.

Bristol (Evans 49093); Hawkins B:126.
Copies: CSt; DeHi; DeWI; DeWin; PHi.

545. LOWTH, ROBERT, 1710–1787.
A short introduction to English grammar: with critical notes. A new ed. By Dr. Lowthe [!] . . . Wilmington, Printed and sold by Bonsal and Niles. Also sold at their bookstore, No. 173, Market-Street, Baltimore, 1800. § viii, 9–140 p.; 12mo.

Evans 37857.
Copies: DeWI; ICN; IaDL; MH; MWA; MdBS; NN; PU.

546. MATHER, COTTON, 1663–1728.
The gospel of justification . . . Wilmington, Printed by Bonsal & Niles, for Molleston Correy [1800]. § 60 p.

Bristol (Evans 49116).
Copies: MB.

547. Mirror of the times, & general advertiser. Vol. 1, no. 13,
      January 1 [–vol. 2, no. 117, December 31, 1800]. Wilming-
ton, Printed by James Wilson, south side of the Upper Market,
High-Street, 1800. § fol.; semi-weekly.

Evans 37971.
Copies: DeGE (microfilm); DeHi; MH; MWA; NHi; NN.

548. The mite of praise. George Washington, the illustrious
      owner of Mount Vernon, was born in Virginia, (and as it is
said) on the 11th day of February, A.D. 1732, old stile. He died on
the 14th of December, A.D. 1799, new stile . . . and for him a nation weeps. Dover, Printed by W. Black, proprietor, 1800. § 11 p.;
8vo.

Evans 37979.
Copies: CSmH; CtY; DLC; NN.

549. The Monitor; or, Wilmington weekly repository. February
      1 [–December, 1800]. Wilmington, Published by W. C.
Smyth, 1800. § fol.; weekly and semi-weekly.

Published weekly until June, 1800, when it became a semi-weekly
with the title *The Monitor, & Wilmington repository*.

Evans 37985.
Copies: DLC; DeHi; DeU (microfilm); MH; MWA; NHi.

550. Moral sketches for young minds . . . Dover, Printed by Wm.
      Black, 1800. § iv, 91 p.; 12mo.

"Originally written in French, by a pen which death has long since
silenced," cf. adv. p. iii.

Evans 37994.
Copies: DeWI.

551. [NELSON, DAVID] 1752–1829.
      An investigation of that false, fabulous and blasphemous
misrepresentation of truth, set forth by Thomas Paine, in his two
volumes, entitled The age of reason, dedicated to the protection of
the United States of America. By a Delaware waggoner; also ded-

icated to the protection of the United States of America: where the Devil, Mahomet, and the heathen philosophers are evidences against Paine's Age of reason. [Wilmington? Peter Brynberg? 1800]. § 192 p.; 8vo.

Advertised by Brynberg in the Wilmington newspaper *Mirror of the times*, no. 70, July 19, 1800; Evans attributes it to the Lancaster, Pa., printers R. & W. Dickson on the basis of an advertisement in the Lancaster *Intelligencer and advertiser* of October, 1800.

Evans 38028.
Copies: DLC; DeWI; MWA; NN.

552.   A new riddle book, or Food for the mind. Containing riddles &c. for the amusement of youth. By Peter Puzzle, Esq. Wilmington, James Wilson, 1800?

From advertisement in: Barbauld, A. L., *Lessons for children*, part II. Wilmington, 1800, p. 44: "In the press and will soon be published, and for sale at J. Wilson's book-store . . ."

No copy known.

553.   OGDEN, JOHN COSENS, 1751–1800.
A tour through Upper and Lower Canada. By John C. Ogden . . . Containing a view of the present state of religion, learning, commerce, agriculture, colonization, customs and manners, among the English, French, and Indian settlements. Second edition. Wilmington, Printed by Bonsal and Niles, for the author, 1800. § 117 p.; 12mo.

"A letter from a gentleman to his friend, descriptive of the different settlements in the province of Upper Canada [dated] New York 20th Nov. 1794": p. 89–117.

Evans 38151.
Copies: CSmH; DGU; DLC; MHi; MWA; NN; PBL; PPAmP; PPL.

554.   PEIRCE, JOHN.
The new American spelling-book: in three parts. Containing, I: Dilworth's Tables . . . The seventh edition. Wilmington, Printed and sold by Peter Brynberg, 1800. § [6], 198 p.; 12mo.

Evans 38206.
Copies: DeWI.

555.   PROTESTANT EPISCOPAL CHURCH IN THE U.S.A.
The book of common prayer, and administration of the sacraments, and other rites and ceremonies of the Church, according to the use of the Protestant Episcopal Church, in the United States of America: together with the Psalter, or Psalms of David. Wilmington, Printed by Peter Brynberg, 1800. § [370], 226, [2] p.; 16mo.

The whole book of Psalms, 226, [2] p. at end.

Evans 38337.
Copies: CSmH; DLC; DeU; DeWI; MdBS; PPPD.

556.   ROCHE, EDWARD, 1754–1821.
A funeral oration, on the death of Gen. George Washington: prepared at the request of the Society of Cincinnati of the State of Delaware, and pronounced at Wilmington, on the 22d day of February, 1800 . . . Wilmington, Printed at the Franklin Press, by James Wilson, 1800. § 15, [1] p.; 8vo.

Evans 38415.
Copies: CSmH; DLC; MBAt; NHi; PHi; PPL.

557.   ROGERS, SAMUEL, 1763–1855.
The pleasures of memory. In two parts. By Samuel Rodgers [!]. Wilmington, Printed at the Franklin Press, by James Wilson, 1800. § 39 p.; 16mo.

Evans 38418.
Copies: DLC; DeHi; DeU; DeWI; MWA; NHi.

558.   [SCOTT, SARAH (ROBINSON)] 1723–1795.
The man of real sensibility; or, The history of Sir George Ellison. Founded on fact . . . Wilmington, Printed and sold by Bonsal & Niles, sold at their book-store, No. 173, Market-Street, Baltimore, 1800. § 72 p.; 24mo.

Evans 38474.
Copies: DLC.

559.   A short address to the voters of Delaware. [Dover? W. Black? 1800]. § 7 p.; 4to.

Dated: Kent County, Spt. 24, 1800, and signed: A Christian federalist.

Bristol (Evans 49147); Hawkins B:138.
Copies: DLC.

560.   [SOCIETY FOR THE SUPPRESSION OF VICE AND IMMO-
        RALITY]
        To the inhabitants of Wilmington, and its neighborhood. [Wilmington, Printed by James Wilson, at the Franklin Press, 1800]. § 7 p.; 4to.

"Signed by order of the Society, Thomas Read, President, Jos. Bringhurst, jun. Sec. 3d mo. (March) 1st, 1800."

Reed 3330.
Copies: DeHi.

561.   TALBOT, CATHERINE, 1721–1770.
        Reflections on the seven days of the week . . . A new edition. Newcastle, Printed by S. & Jno. Adams, 1800. § 36 p.; 12mo.

Evans 38601.
Copies: MWA.

562.   To the people of Cecil. No. I–III. Wilmington, Printed at the Franklin Press, by J. Wilson, 1800. § 3 no. in 1.; 8vo.

Three Democratic pamphlets of the campaign of 1800, dated at Elkton, Sept. 3, 15, 26, 1800. Signed: A voter.

Evans 38655.
Copies: DLC.

563.   U.S. PRESIDENT.
        President's speech! On Saturday the 22d November, at 12 o'clock, the President met both houses of Congress . . . [Wilmington, Printed by James Wilson, 1800]. § Broadside.

John Adams, President.

Evans 38802.
Copies: DeHi.

564.   The United States' almanac, or the North-American cal-
ander [!]; for the year of our Lord 1801 . . . Wilmington,
Printed and sold wholesale by James Adams, north-side of the
Upper-Market [1800]. § [36] p.; 12mo.

Drake 1411.
Copies: DeHi; DeWI.

565.   VAUGHAN, JOHN, 1775–1807.
The valedictory lecture, delivered before the Philosophical
Society of Delaware . . . Wilmington, Printed at the Franklin Press,
by James Wilson, 1800. § 36 p.; 12mo.

At end of most copies is bound his *Chemical syllabus*, 21 p., with
dedication dated: Wilmington, November 20, 1799.

Evans 38924.
Copies: CtY; DeGE; DeHi; DeWI; NHi; NN; PHi (now in PPL);
PPAmP.

566.   The Wilmingtoniad, or A touch at the times. A dialogue . . .
Wilmington, Printed at the Franklin Press by James Wilson, 1800. § 19 p.; 16mo.

Reprint from the *Mirror of the times*, attributed to John Vaughan or
James Wilson by Evans, and to Joseph Bringhurst on the basis of
a manuscript note on one of the copies.

Evans 39115.
Copies: DLC; De (photocopy); DeHi; DeU (photocopy).

INDEX OF PRINTERS, PUBLISHERS
AND BOOKSELLERS

(Active in Wilmington, unless otherwise indicated)

Numbers refer to entries

Dickson, R. & W. (Lancaster, Pa.), 551n

Franklin Press, 518, 524, 525, 530, 532, 541, 556, 557, 560, 562, 565, 566

Jess, Zachariah, 512, 514
Johnson, B., 540
Johnson, B. & J., 540
Johnson, Joseph, 386, 387, 394, 405, 412, 415, 422, 424, 445, 479, 540
Johnson, Joseph, and Co., 386
Johnson and Preston, 445, 479

Keatinge, George (Baltimore), 363n, 374
Killen, Jacob A., and Co., 188, 189, 190, 191, 192, 193, 195, 196, 197, 204, 207, 208, 214, 232
Killen, Jacob Allee, 188, 189, 190, 191, 192, 193, 195, 196, 197, 198, 204, 205, 206, 207, 208, 210, 214, 230, 232

Mirror book-store and printing-office, 523

Neilson, David, 69

Niles, Hezekiah, 375, 391, 404, 423, 464, 467, 469n, 470, 471, 499, 505, 507, 511, 512, 514, 516, 517, 519, 520, 526, 528, 529, 533, 544, 545, 546, 553, 558

Pattillo, Henry, 248
Preston, 445, 479

Smyth, William Catherwood, 344, 354, 361, 371, 402n, 440, 442, 457, 477, 487, 494, 496, 549
Starr, Caleb, 372n, 374n, 376, 383, 402

Thompson, J., 385

Vaughan, John, 505
Vaughan & Coleman, 505

Weems, Mason Locke, 357, 377
Wilson, James, 389, 393, 406, 416, 419, 424, 469, 498, 513, 518, 523, 524, 525, 530, 532, 541, 543, 547, 552, 556, 557, 560, 562, 563, 565, 566
Wilson, William (Philadelphia), 40

Zane, Jonathan (Philadelphia), 40

AUTHOR AND TITLE INDEX

Numbers refer to entries

199

201

tion, 1791–1792, 306n, 308, 309, 310

Delaware. General Assembly, 98, 99, 106, 108, 113, 114, 115, 123, 130, 131, 132, 137, 138, 139, 140, 141, 150, 151, 152, 168, 169, 180, 194, 195, 196, 197, 207, 208, 222, 223, 224, 240, 241, 242, 260, 261, 277, 278, 279, 293, 294, 313, 352, 370, 398, 437, 484, 503, 536

Delaware. General Assembly. House, 107, 128, 163, 164, 165, 166, 178, 188, 189, 190, 191, 204, 205, 206, 217, 218, 219, 237, 238, 239, 257, 258, 259, 275, 276, 290, 291, 292, 311, 328, 329, 349, 350, 368, 395, 396, 432, 433, 482, 500, 534

Delaware. General Assembly. Senate, 220, 221, 312, 330, 331, 351, 369, 397, 434, 435, 483, 501, 535

Delaware. Governor, 100, 110, 111, 120, 121, 122, 129, 135, 136, 144, 145, 146, 147, 167, 179, 192, 193

Delaware. Laws, 101, 102, 108, 112, 113, 114, 115, 116, 123, 130, 131, 132, 137, 138, 139, 140, 141, 148, 149, 150, 151, 152, 153, 154, 155, 156, 157, 168, 169, 180, 181, 194, 195, 196, 197, 207, 208, 222, 223, 224, 240, 241, 242, 260, 261, 277, 278, 279, 293, 294, 313, 332, 333, 334, 352, 370, 398, 399, 400, 436, 437, 438, 484, 485, 502, 503, 536

Delaware. Legislative Council, see: Delaware. General Assembly. Senate

Delaware. Lt. Governor, 158

Delaware. Militia, 353

Delaware. Supreme Court, 124

The Delaware almanack, or Eastern-Shore calendar, 225, 252, 262, 270, 287

The Delaware and Eastern-Shore advertiser, 354, 371, 401, 439, 486, 504

The Delaware courant, and weekly advertiser, 203

The Delaware courant, and Wilmington advertiser, 209, 226

The Delaware gazette, 198, 210, 263, 295, 314, 335, 355, 372, 402, 440, 441, 487, 496, 505

The Delaware gazette; or The Faithful centinel, 198n, 227, 243

The Delaware gazette, and general advertiser, 263n, 280

Delaware laws, see: Delaware. Laws

The Delaware pocket almanac, 265

Delaware State Mills, 410

Delaware State, November 15, 1784, 181

Delaware State, ss., 124, 193

The Delaware State to, 111

A Delaware waggoner, 551

The delusions of the heart, 254

Democratic Party of Kent County, 518n

A descant on the command, Mat. xxviii. 19, 20, 91

Descriptive, picturesque and instructive passages, 408, 452

A dialogue, spoken at opening the

206

WITHDRAWAL